# THE MOST SACRED FREEDOM

THE McDONALD
CENTER FOR
AMERICA'S FOUNDING
PRINCIPLES

MERCER
UNIVERSITY

The A. V. Elliott Conference Series

The Thomas C. and Ramona E. McDonald Center
for America's Founding Principles

Guided by James Madison's maxim that "a well-instructed people alone can be permanently a free people," the McDonald Center exists to promote the study of the great texts and ideas that have shaped our regime and fostered liberal learning.
Directors
Will R. Jordan
Charlotte C. S. Thomas

Published Volumes
Charlotte C. S. Thomas, ed., *No Greater Monster nor Miracle than Myself: The Political Philosophy of Michel de Montaigne*

Charlotte C. S. Thomas, ed., *Of Sympathy and Selfishness: The Moral and Political Philosophy of Adam Smith*

# THE MOST SACRED FREEDOM

*Religious Liberty in the History of
Philosophy and America's Founding*

Edited by

Will R. Jordan and Charlotte C.S. Thomas

Mercer University Press | Macon, Georgia

2016

MUP/ P524

© 2016 by Mercer University Press
Published by Mercer University Press
1501 Mercer University Drive
Macon, Georgia 31207
All rights reserved

9 8 7 6 5 4 3 2 1

Books published by Mercer University Press are printed on acid-free paper that meets the requirements of the American National Standard for Information Sciences—Permanence of Paper for Printed Library Materials.

ISBN     978-0-88146-563-1
Cataloging-in-Publication Data is available from the Library of Congress

MERCER UNIVERSITY PRESS

*Endowed by*

TOM WATSON BROWN
*and*
THE WATSON-BROWN FOUNDATION, INC.

# CONTENTS

Contributors / vi
Acknowledgments / vii

Introduction | *Will R. Jordan* / 1

Part I  Religious Liberty in the Western Tradition
1. Religion and Liberty in Neglected Great Works of the Ancient Near East | *Steven Grosby* / 9
2. Faction against Faction: Emperor Julian on Religious Tolerance | *Jeremiah H. Russell* / 35
3. Calvert, Williams, and Locke: Three Foundations for Religious Toleration in America | *Maura Jane Farrelly* / 63
4. Religion and Social Unity: Another Rousseauian Paradox | *Daniel Cullen* / 87

Part II  Religious Liberty and the American Founding
5. The Shifting Walls of Separation Between Church and State in the United States | *John Witte, Jr.* / 103
6. The American Founders and the Problem of Civil Religion: Truth and Utility | *Scott Yenor* / 121
7. The Founders, Hobby Lobby and the HHS Mandate | *David Ramsey* / 133
8. What Sort of God Calls for Liberty of Conscience? | *Michael Novak* / 159

Index / 175

# CONTRIBUTORS

**Daniel Cullen**—Associate Professor of Political Science, Co-Director of the Project for the Study of Liberal Democracy, Rhodes College, Memphis, Tennessee

**Maura Jane Farrelly**—Associate Professor of American Studies, Director of the Journalism Program, Brandeis University, Waltham, Massachusetts

**Steven Grosby**—Professor of Religion, Clemson University, Clemson, South Carolina

**Will R. Jordan**—Associate Professor of Political Science, Co-Director of the McDonald Center for America's Founding Principles, Mercer University, Macon, Georgia

**Michael Novak**—Author, Philosopher, Theologian, and Diplomat; Trustee and Visiting Professor, Ave Maria University, Ave Maria, Florida

**David Ramsey**—Assistant Professor of Government, University of West Florida, Pensacola, Florida

**Jeremiah H. Russell**—Assistant Professor of Political Science, Jacksonville State University, Jacksonville, Alabama

**Charlotte C.S. Thomas**—Professor of Philosophy, Co-Director of the McDonald Center for America's Founding Principles, Director of the Philosophy, Politics, and Economics Program, Mercer University, Macon, Georgia

**John Witte, Jr.**—Robert W. Woodruff Professor of Law, McDonald Distinguished Professor, and Director of the Center for the Study of Law and Religion, Emory University, Atlanta, Georgia

**Scott Yenor**—Professor of Political Science, Boise State University, Boise, Idaho

# ACKNOWLEDGMENTS

This collection of essays is based on the 2014 A.V. Elliott Conference on Great Books and Ideas, the 7th annual conference sponsored by the Thomas C. and Ramona E. McDonald Center for America's Founding Principles.

The McDonald Center for America's Founding Principles began as a small conference in the spring of 2008. It secured initial funding that summer through Mercer University's Academic Initiatives Monetary (AIM) fund and has grown substantially each year. Neither this volume, nor the conference, nor any of the other important work now done by the McDonald Center would have been possible without the foresight of Mercer President William D. Underwood, the confidence of the AIM committee, the support of the College of Liberal Arts Dean Lake Lambert, and the entrepreneurial spirit of the Center's founders.

In the spring of 2013, the McDonald Center received a generous endowment from Mr. A.V. Elliott, for whom our annual conference is now named. Also in 2013, Thomas and Ramona McDonald endowed all of the Center's work, and with it they gave us their name. We are, and always will be, in deep debt to the Elliotts and McDonalds for their support.

Our 2014 Elliott conference on religious liberty was a gathering of scholars on Mercer's main campus in Macon, Georgia. It was also the culmination of a year-long study of religious liberty by Mercer faculty and students meeting in a reading group. We are grateful to all of the participants in that project. Each of them contributed significantly to the excellent conversation that animated our conference and inspired this volume of essays. So, thank you, Carl Findley, Craig McMahan, David Oedel, J. Thomas Scott, Brandon Brock, Jackson Brown, Colleen Closson, Connor Cosenza, Ronnie Davis, Shelby Hall, Patrick Jolley, Anna Mae Kersey, Ethan Parrish, Raymond Partolan, Precious Patterson, Hetu Shah, and Timothy Walker. We are also grateful to the Apgar Foundation for providing a generous grant to support the work of this reading group, and to Vincent Phillip Munoz and Daniel Dreisbach for visiting campus to share their insight and wisdom with our student and faculty participants.

We are sincerely thankful to Michael Novak, John Witte Jr, Daniel Cullen, Maura Jane Farrelly, Steven Grosby, David Ramsey, Jeremiah H. Russell, and Scott Yenor for presenting their scholarly work at the Elliott Conference, for interacting so thoughtfully with our students, and for allowing us to include their essays in this volume. It was a lovely conference, and these scholars set the tone with a perfect balance of seriousness of purpose and warm collegiality. We would also like to thank our undergraduate student panelists, who showed great ambition and courage by sharing their research with all who attended the Elliott Conference: Jackson Brown, Ronnie Davis, Patrick Jolley, and Anna Mae Kersey. Anna Bates deserves special thanks for her editorial assistance on this volume, especially for her work on the index.

Will Jordan, in particular, would like to thank his wife, Anissa, for making possible his work with the Center, and his sons, Evan and Alex, for reminding him of what is at stake in preserving and extending the great principles of liberty, virtue, and justice that undergird our regime. It has also been his great pleasure to work with Charlotte Thomas on all things related to the McDonald Center over the past eight years.

Charlotte Thomas thanks her children, Francis and Isaiah, for sharing her with Mercer, as well as her parents, who reluctantly dropped her off on College Street all those years ago. She is deeply grateful for the opportunity to do this good work, and to have the chance to collaborate with Will Jordan, who is such a wonderful partner in it.

# INTRODUCTION

## Will R. Jordan

The essays in this volume were originally prepared for the 2014 A.V. Elliott Conference on Great Books and Ideas at Mercer University, held in early April of that year. At the time, the country was waiting anxiously for the Supreme Court to hand down its decision in *Burwell v. Hobby Lobby*, determining whether or not a for-profit corporation might claim an exception, on religious liberty grounds, to certain provisions of the Affordable Care Act mandating coverage of contraception for female employees. Any academic conference on religious liberty conducted in the spring of 2014 was likely to be dominated by considerations of this case.[1] Likewise, any edited volume produced from such a conference would likely be of interest only to those who were interested in the *Hobby Lobby* decision, and therefore of diminishing value as the twists and turns of First Amendment jurisprudence invariably open up new and different questions. Such a volume would quickly become a historic or scholarly artifact rather than a resource that might help inform and guide our thinking today as well as tomorrow.

Fortunately, this volume manages to avoid this trap. The A.V. Elliott Conference is consciously dedicated to exploring the books and ideas that have been most influential in shaping the foundations of the American regime. The contributors were asked simply to prepare essays that considered either the American founders' conceptions of religious liberty or any antecedent thinkers in the tradition who might have informed the founders' views. While this

---

[1] In fact, the first question posed to our opening speaker, John Witte Jr., came from Mercer University President William Underwood, who asked Professor Witte to predict the outcome of the *Hobby Lobby* decision. To his credit, Professor Witte correctly predicted the 5-4 decision in favor of Hobby Lobby.

procedure appears to eschew the "timely" and "current," it is designed to reach to those fundamental issues and questions that, in fact, extend beyond the fleeting controversies of the moment. At least one of the essays in this volume explicitly addresses the specifics of the *Hobby Lobby* case. More importantly, however, they together explore the idea of religious liberty in its political, moral, philosophical, and theological dimensions, thereby helping us grasp more fully the ends, preconditions, and essential challenges of securing this most sacred freedom.

The book is organized into two parts. The first includes four chapters and considers important texts and historical figures in the Western tradition that inform our understanding of religious liberty. Steven Grosby, in "Religion and Liberty in Neglected Great Works of the Ancient Near East," compares the biblical story of the flood to the earlier, Mesopotamian account found in the *Atra-Ḫasīs*. He does so not to explore matters of influence or historical relation, but to consider essential thematic differences between the works. He finds that, when compared to the *Atra-Ḫasīs*, the Genesis account "provides an optimistic framework for human existence," thereby creating the hopeful psychological preconditions necessary for the development of liberty. It is fitting that the volume opens by considering how human society, and especially its prospect for freedom, is shaped by our conceptions of the cosmos and of man's relationship with God. This is a subject to which we will return in the final chapter of the book.

In "Faction against Faction: Emperor Julian on Religious Tolerance," Jeremiah H. Russell examines the political thought and practice of one of history's more enigmatic figures. The chapter seeks to resolve the apparent contradiction that one of the first great programs of religious toleration after the rise of Christianity was made by a noted antagonist to the faith—Emperor Julian, the Apostate. Against modern apologists, Russell argues that Julian had no principled commitment to toleration, but instead "used toleration as a mechanism to neutralize, if not subvert, Christianity by pitting the various factions within the faith against one another." After examining in detail Julian's various political machinations, Russell concludes that Julian's subversive scheme to neutralize the power of Christianity was, indeed, ahead of its time, and can be glimpsed in some of the major Enlightenment defenses of religious toleration. The chapter invites us to reconsider the widely accepted assumption that toleration serves equally well both civic and religious interests.

Maura Jane Farrelly's chapter takes up the subject of religious toleration by emphasizing its essential difference from a more comprehensive religious liberty. Unlike religious toleration, which merely indulges error, full religious liberty demands that the public "skirt the issue of whether there is a right answer to the God question." She examines the writings of three major 17th century defenders of religious toleration—Roger Williams, Cecilius Calvert, and John Locke—and concludes that only Locke's account is compatible with a complete move to religious liberty. The key is to be found in Locke's epistemology, with his claim that our "obscure and relative" ideas, such as those of God, cannot be adequately transmitted to others and therefore constitute an "inappropriate foundation for politics." We see here that religious liberty might depend not only on the conception of God we hold, but on a certain philosophical understanding of that conception.

The final chapter of Part I, Daniel Cullen's "Religion and Social Unity: Another Rousseauian Paradox," suggests that most contemporary debate about the proper role of religion in society pits those who consider religion an inappropriate source of political legitimacy—and therefore, like Farrelly's Locke, make it a matter of merely private concern—against those who embrace similar democratic and secular principles of political legitimacy but nonetheless believe that religion is an indispensible support for public life. Cullen refers to these two camps as "neutralist liberals" and "conservative liberals." His essay explores the political thought of Jean-Jacques Rousseau in order to elucidate how Rousseau's use of civil religion in some ways acknowledges the concerns of both groups. In Cullen's account, Rousseau believes "legitimate law can only arise from the consent of the people subject to it, but if the law is not sanctified, that is, regarded as transcending the people, it will lack moral force and practical efficacy." Cullen does not regard Rousseau as having solved this dilemma, but rather praises him for revealing a permanent tension in the nature of modern democratic life.

The book's second part focuses more narrowly on the thought of the American founders and the characteristics of the U.S. constitutional order with respect to religious liberty. John Witte Jr. gives us a marvelous overview of how the core principle of separation of church and state has been understood in America. He identifies "five distinct understandings of separation of church and state at work in the American founding era," and suggests that one in particular—the "strict separation" of religion from all public life—has grown unduly prominent in recent Supreme Court decisions. Witte concludes that separation of church and state is a valuable constitutional ideal only so long as it remains in balance with other founding principles of religious freedom, including "liberty of conscience, freedom of religious exercise, [and] religious equality of a plurality of peaceable faiths." When it is upheld in exclusion of these other goods, as the Supreme Court has lately been tempted to do, strict separation of church and state can serve to undermine the core promise of religious liberty.

In his chapter "The American Founders and the Problem of Civil Religion," Scott Yenor picks up, in part, where Daniel Cullen left off. Yenor argues that the founders envisioned a kind of "weak" civil religion, where religion is praised for its usefulness in cultivating the necessary moral foundation to support republican self-government. He compares the founders to Alexis de Tocqueville in this respect. Yenor suggests, however, that Tocqueville's more complete and nuanced discussion of religion reveals the limits of the founders' thinking. Tocqueville and Yenor fear that religion defended only for its utility will be unable to resist the natural democratic tendency to exalt human power beyond limits. Once religion's truth matters less than its utility, and "modern people provide a modern account for the religious psychology, doctrinal indifference cannot resist the movements of the democratic heart." We are invited here to question the effectiveness of a merely instrumental defense of religion's role in modern life.

David Ramsey's "The Founders, Hobby Lobby and the HHS Mandate," provides the most direct reflection on the political and judicial controversies swirling in the spring of 2014. While doing so, Ramsey offers a wide-ranging discussion of the constitutional questions surrounding "religious liberty, corporate personhood, and the 'quasi-legislative, quasi-judicial' role of administrative and regulatory agencies." At the end, what impresses Ramsey most about the Court's decision in *Burwell v. Hobby Lobby* is the extreme narrowness of its holding and its surprising lack of a coherent and full-throated defense of religious liberty. He observes that "one reason for the enduring popularity of our First Amendment is that it provides each of us as citizens with an account of what the truth is like, and how it is to be found. Any Court which requires truth-seeking to yield to fact-telling is in sore need of rediscovering the authentic meaning of the First Amendment." It seems, then, that Ramsey finds the Court deficient in taking seriously some of the foundational questions raised in this volume.

The book closes with a lovely essay by Michael Novak. Taking up the issue broached in the first chapter, Novak asks "What Sort of God Calls for Liberty of Conscience?" One god he is certain does not make such a call is the god of deism, "usually described as impersonal, unfeeling, and indifferent to the individual conscience. Such a god is unmoved by the human fate even of the noble and the heroic." Novak is especially troubled, therefore, that modern historians have spread the falsehood that most of the American founders were deists. Focusing on the central deist premise that "there is no special providence; no miracles or divine interventions intrude upon the lawful natural order," Novak demonstrates that deism is wholly inconsistent with the public acts and documents of the founding generation. More fundamentally, he argues that the very idea of liberty of conscience, especially as the founders conceived it, only makes sense in the context of a duty to "a Living God Who is Spirit and Truth, an undeceivable Reader of Human hearts." Novak counsels gratitude for the fact that, since this Judeo-Christian God is the God of all, Jews and Christians can make a "principled argument for defending the liberties [even] of those who reject God and excuse themselves from His friendship."

We therefore begin with hope and end with gratitude. These seem fitting bookends when studying this first and most sacred freedom. Between the two sentiments, we consider the theological and epistemological preconditions of religious liberty, some of the chief challenges to securing this liberty, the problematic but necessary role of religion in a free society, and the constitutional framework that has been handed down to us to help face these challenges. It is our hope that the book is able to transcend the narrow passions of today and therefore might be of some use even for the challenges to come.

# PART I

# RELIGIOUS LIBERTY IN THE WESTERN TRADITION

I

# RELIGION AND LIBERTY IN NEGLECTED GREAT WORKS OF THE ANCIENT NEAR EAST

*Steven Grosby*

What can we learn from a number of neglected "great works" from the ancient Near East about the relation between religion and liberty? One might think that the answer to this question is that there is very little to be learned; but, as we shall see, that is not so. Why is it important that these works be no longer neglected by programs orientated primarily to undergraduates? The following remarks are intended to serve as an introductory attempt to address these questions.

At first glance the very idea of a neglected great work appears as something of a paradox; for if a work is deemed to be great, how could it be neglected? The significance of this apparent paradox is lessened once we remember that the category of the great works is a product of tradition: the result of a centuries-long practice of discriminating worthy from less worthy. The criterion of worthiness revolves around the extent to which a particular work touches upon in an illuminating way those problems central to our existence, for example, the relation between man and woman, the relation between the individual and his or her society, and the relation between the individual and the cosmos, including our understanding of death.

As we know, for any tradition—in this case, the determination of the great works of our civilization—to remain relevant, it must be taken up into the life of the current generation.[1] If it isn't, sooner or

---

[1] On tradition and its reception, see T.S. Eliot, "Tradition and Individual Talent" in *Selected Essays* (New York: Harcourt, Brace & World,

later the tradition will not even be the dead hand of the past on the present, because it will simply be ignored. Precisely here, however, we encounter a complication. When the current generation acknowledges the tradition of the great works, some degree of modification in the determination of what those great works are is unavoidable because the act of acknowledgment—the reception of the tradition—will always be influenced by the preoccupations of the current generation. This unavoidable modification of the tradition is the price, if you will, that the past must pay for being taken up into the life of the present. Thus, the consequence of the reception of the tradition of the great works by the current generation is that the determination of those works deemed to be great is not immutable. There is an unavoidable shifting, as one work is now recognized to be more important or worthy of attention than another work; or a relatively new work, having been judged to be great, takes its place within the tradition. To give only a few of the many examples of this unavoidable re-evaluation of what are the great works: why should Thucydides' *History of the Peloponnesian War* be read as a great work, when doing so often results in the neglect of Herodotus' *The History*? What prejudices are at play in such an evaluation? Are the prejudices warranted or unwarranted? And are we not today witnessing increasing neglect of a work that was once rightly recognized to be important to the Western tradition, Hesiod's *Theogony*?

But prejudices there are. It is curious that many programs of the "Great Works" or "Great Ideas" proceed as if the Garden of Eden must have been located somewhere in the vicinity of Athens. While we never will know the location of the Garden, we can be sure it wasn't anywhere in Greece. The obvious result of this prejudice, whether intended or not, in proceeding this way is only to reinforce the unwarranted neglect of the great works of the Ancient Near East. The purpose of the ensuing, brief remarks is to clarify why this

---

1960), 3-11; Edward Shils, *Tradition* (Chicago: University of Chicago Press, 1981).

neglect is a mistake. In doing so, I hope to contribute modestly to modifying the reception of the tradition of the "Great Works."

## Mesopotamia: The *Atra-Ḫasīs*

That there are other accounts of a world-encompassing flood beyond what appears in the biblical account of Genesis 6-9 is generally acknowledged. However, rarely is the *Atra-Ḫasīs*, the Mesopotamian story of the flood, read in programs devoted to the Great Works.[2] This is a mistake for a number of reasons.

Given the probable date for the Akkadian composition of the *Atra-Ḫasīs* to be sometime around 1600 B.C.E., we are most likely dealing with a Mesopotamian account of the flood that predates the biblical account.[3] Furthermore, as archaeologists have discovered copies of the *Atra-Ḫasīs* at various places throughout the ancient Near East, including at Ras Shamra, the location of the ancient port of Ugarit on the Mediterranean coast of modern Syria, approximately 150 to 200 miles from Israel, we know that those copies circulated throughout the ancient Near East. Given that circulation, including relatively near to the land of ancient Israel, it is reasonable to pose the possibility that the earlier Mesopotamian account may have influenced the composition of the biblical account. So the argument has been ever since George Smith delivered a paper on the Mesopotamian account of the flood to the Society of Biblical Archaeology in 1872.

---

[2] For the scholarly edition, W.G. Lambert and A.R. Millard, *Atra-Ḫasīs: The Babylonian Story of the Flood, with the Sumerian Flood Story by M. Civil* (Oxford: Oxford University Press, 1969), affordably republished and available today by Eisenbrauns (1999). For a translation and edition appropriate for undergraduates, as the extant partial versions have been combined for the purpose of coherence, see Benjamin R. Foster, *From Ancient Days: Myths, Tales and Poetry of Ancient Mesopotamia* (Bethesda, CDL Press: 1995), 52-77.

[3] For this date of composition, see Lambert and Millard, 14, 23.

## THE MOST SACRED FREEDOM

Initially, the discovery of the *Atra-Ḫasīs* was understood to have provided a confirmation of the historical fact of a world-encompassing flood as recounted in the biblical account. After all, Atra-Ḫasīs is told by his god, Enki, about the impending flood, to build an ark, and to take on it different kinds of animals and birds. When the rain ceases, he successively sends out three birds to find out if there is dry land; and then once on land, he, like Noah, makes a sacrifice, presumably to the god Enki.[4] However, needless to say, it did not take long for a different understanding of the relation of the biblical account to the Mesopotamian to emerge, namely, that the biblical account was derivative of the Mesopotamian.[5]

It should go without saying that it is necessary for students to know of the probable relation between the *Atra-Ḫasīs* and the biblical account of the flood, irrespective of whatever theological problems might arise. Our ethical obligations as university professors require no less. Nevertheless, however necessary it is to note the similarities between the two accounts, it is considerably more important for students to observe the differences between them and, then, ponder the significance of those differences; for it is there where we come upon reasons enough to consider the *Atra-Ḫasīs* worthy of being included in the tradition of "great works," including the relation between religion and liberty. By the differences between the two accounts, I am not referring to such facts as the rain lasting for "seven days and seven nights" in the Mesopotamian account, while in

---

[4] We do not know for certain if the sending out of three birds appeared in the *Atra-Ḫasīs* because there is unfortunately a gap of about sixty lines in the tablet; but given that the birds are sent out in the flood account in the *Epic of Gilgamesh*, one assumes it was contained in that gap of the missing lines.

[5] The dispute over the relation of the two accounts is a part of what is known as the "Babel/Bible" controversy; for an overview, see Mogens Trolle Larsen, "The 'Babel/Bible' Controversy and Its Aftermath" in Jack M. Sasson, ed., *Civilizations of the Ancient Near East* (Peabody: Hendrickson, 2000), 95-106.

Genesis it rains "for forty days and forty nights."[6] Those kinds of differences are obvious enough, but clearly they have no bearing on the central problems of our existence and specifically the relation between religion and liberty. As we shall see, the differences between the two accounts are so important that consideration of the likelihood that the Mesopotamian account of the flood influenced the composition of the biblical account recedes in significance.

The differences between the two accounts, so compelling that they warrant attention to *Atra-Ḫasīs*, are apparent at the most fundamental level: the description of the very nature of human existence. The biblical account, however ambiguous, but richly so, describes humanity as having being created "in the image of God" (Genesis 1:27). Furthermore, we find in the Genesis account of the creation of humanity a blessing of humanity to "be fruitful and multiply" and to make the earth one's own (Genesis 1:28). And likely indicating a compositional unity of Genesis 1-9, both of these statements of, respectively, what humanity is and what it should do in Genesis 1 are repeated in the description of the new Adam, Noah, as the conclusion to the biblical account of the flood (Genesis 9:6; 9:1, 7). For these reasons we conclude that the biblical account provides an optimistic framework for human existence: an orderly creation of the cosmos that provides hope for humanity by including 1) a description of some kind of existential relation between the deity and humanity through the idiom of humanity having been made in the "image of God," and 2) a framework of activity linking humanity and the deity through a covenant (Genesis 6:18, 9:9) that contains the expectation of what humanity should do: to procreate and be productive in the completion of the world. We do not find in the Genesis account of the creation of humanity a fundamental denial of earthly life.

In contrast, we find a provocatively different description of human existence in the *Atra-Ḫasīs*. There, human beings are described as having been created for only one reason: to bear the

---

[6] Foster, p. 74, line 139; see also p. 71, line 33; Genesis 7:4, 12, 17.

burden of the forced labor of the "Igigi-gods," the lower or junior gods, from having to dig the river-beds of the Tigris and Euphrates and the canals.[7] This pessimistic, thematic motif for why humanity exists is not limited in the Mesopotamian literature to the *Atra-Ḫasīs*; for in the Babylonian epic of creation, the *Enuma Eliš*, Marduk, the emergent king of the Babylonian pantheon, resolves to create humankind also to "bear the gods' burden so that they (the gods) may rest."[8] Thus, even though in both the *Atra-Ḫasīs* and the *Enuma Eliš* humanity is described as having been created out of a combination of clay and the blood of a slaughtered deity, indicating perhaps some divine aspect to human existence, we nonetheless conclude that, in contrast to the biblical account, the Mesopotamian understanding of the existence of humanity and its place in the cosmos is decisively pessimistic.[9]

Not surprisingly, other expressions of the contrast between the optimism of the biblical account and the pessimism of the Mesopotamian account of humanity's place and purpose in the cosmos are found. In the biblical account, the reason for the flood is God's judgment that the earth had become corrupt as a result of humanity's wickedness (Genesis 6:5, 12; 8:21). This biblical evaluation of human nature is not to be judged as thoroughly pessimistic; rather, the wickedness or evil in the thought of humanity is seen as a corruption that is capable of being responded to and dealt with. In fact, the response to the corruption marks the conclusion to the biblical account of the flood: the introduction of the legal stipulation against wanton murder as an initial means to constrain the wickedness of humanity. The constraint is conveyed through the deity's covenant with Noah:

---

[7] Foster, p. 52, line 6; p. 53, lines 20-25; pp. 57-58.

[8] Foster, p. 38, line 8. Foster (1995) conveniently includes all of the Mesopotamian works, the *Enuma Eliš*, the *Atra-Ḫasīs*, the so-called "Babylonian Theodicy," and the "Poem of a Righteous Sufferer," referred to in this chapter.

[9] For the creation of humanity in the *Enuma Eliš*, Foster, pp. 38-39; in the *Atra-Ḫasīs*, pp. 58-59.

Whoever sheds the blood of a human,
By a human shall that person's blood be shed;
for in his image
did God make humankind.
Be fruitful, then, and increase; abound on the earth and increase on it.
(Genesis 9:6-7)

To the extent that Noah is the new Adam—the literary evidence for understanding Noah this way is compelling—what is different with this "second creation" after the flood is the introduction of the recognition of the necessity to address the wicked character of humanity by limiting the scope of human action through the innovation of this legal stipulation against wanton murder.[10] Furthermore and of considerable importance, even though the wickedness of humanity is twice noted (Genesis 6:5, 8:21), the conclusion to the biblical account of the flood maintains the hopeful optimism of Genesis 1, by twice repeating the commandment initially given to Adam but now given to Noah, "Be fruitful, then, and increase; abound on the earth and increase on it" (Genesis 9:1, 7).

The Mesopotamian account of the flood lacks entirely the biblical account's moral axis and the meaningful order of the cosmos that it implies. The absence of a moral axis in the *Atra-Ḥasīs* is seen in both its reason for the flood and its conclusion to it. What is that reason for the flood in the Mesopotamian account? Twelve hundred years after the creation of humanity, the human population had increased so much that "the land was bellowing like a bull," the result of which was that the god Enlil, the chief god of the pantheon in the *Atra-Ḥasīs*,

---

[10] The covenant with Noah constrains not only humanity from wanton murder but also the deity from destroying life through a second flood, Genesis 9:8-15, thereby indicating the "two-sided" structure of the covenantal relation; see below.

heard their clamor
and said to the great gods,
"the clamor of humanity has become burdensome to me,
I am losing sleep . . . let there be plague."[11]

So, rather than, as in the biblical account, humanity being told "to be fruitful and multiply" and "to master [or complete] the earth," those very hope-bearing expectations of human fertility and innovative activity arouse, in the *Atra-Ḫasīs*, the destructive fury of Enlil. This Mesopotamian description of divine hostility to humanity takes place entirely in naturalistic terms: Enlil is deprived of his sleep because of the noise created by the existence of too many humans.

The conclusion to the *Atra-Ḫasīs* is also devoid of any moral axis as it is entirely aetiological. Although Enlil eventually tolerates, as a consequence of a god's deception, the continued existence of humanity, Enki, the god who deceived Enlil by safeguarding human life by warning Atra-Ḫasīs, is forced to come up with plans to reduce the size of the human population. He does so by making sure that not only would death be a part of the human condition, but also that there be both infertility for some women and infant mortality to "cut down childbirth."[12] True enough, the biblical account also contains an aetiological motif to account for the human life-span, "Then the LORD said, 'My spirit [or breath, *rûaḥ*] shall not abide in humans forever, for they are flesh; their days shall be one hundred twenty years'" (Genesis 6:3). Be that as it may, entirely absent in the *Atra-Ḫasīs*, but dominating the conclusion of the biblical account of the flood, is the recognition of the sanctity of all life, as conveyed in the above quotation, Genesis 9:6-7.

The differences between the two accounts serve to illuminate the optimistic emphasis in the biblical story of the flood on how life is to be viewed: all life is sacred, humans are to procreate, and they are to

---

[11] Foster, p. 62, lines 343-51.
[12] Foster, pp. 76-77.

complete the creation of the world through their activity, now morally and legally constrained by the injunction not to murder. In contrast, in the *Atra-Ḥasīs*, humanity suffers a pessimistic sentence of a life of drudgery, and what life there is must never become abundant, but rather reduced. The significance of this contrast provides reason enough for careful attention to the *Atra-Ḥasīs* in programs devoted to the "great works" or "great ideas." There is, however, another reason that has not yet been brought to the surface of these remarks.

We are understandably accustomed to view liberty in the Western tradition in terms of institutional differentiation: for example, the American separation between Church and State or the independence of the judiciary necessary for the rule of law, and a legal framework recognizing private property, both for the individual and the corporation. In doing so, we recognize a limit to the authority and scope of activity of the State that allows for the liberty of both the individual and various associations of individuals. A focus on the relation between institutional and legal frameworks, on the one hand, and liberty, on the other, is proper.

However, the views on this relation found in the various Western religious traditions are actually quite complicated. For example, there are differences over how to view the State among various, Christian denominations.[13] To take another example that indicates how complicated these matters are: if one restricts oneself entirely to the New Testament, one can only wonder what actually is the Christian stance toward private property, the accumulation of wealth, and even the family. These matters are, of course, dealt with differently in the Hebrew Bible. In any event, in these brief remarks, I take for granted that institutional differentiation and the legal

---

[13] Here, Ernst Troeltsch, *The Social Teachings of the Christian Churches* (George Allen & Unwin, 1931) remains valuable. For a recent, well-written and illuminating treatment of Catholicism's views on private property and commercial relations, see Sam Gregg, *Tea Party Catholic: The Catholic Case for Limited Government, a Free Economy, and Human Flourishing* (Crossroads, 2013).

relations of private property are crucial for liberty. I also overlook a number of complications by readily acknowledging the important contribution of the history of Christianity to the Western conception of liberty.[14] Nevertheless, while not for a moment doubting the significance of these factors for liberty, I wish to draw attention to another factor that does not receive the attention that it deserves.

It is difficult to see how liberty can be fostered in a pessimistic mental environment. If the individual (or a group of individuals) is to take initiative, to experiment, and to take risk in the face of uncertainty, there must be some kind of optimistic assumption that the individual does so with the expectation that his or her lot in life can be improved. Perhaps this mental environment as a necessary prerequisite for liberty is easily overlooked, as we take it for granted. But we take it for granted because the tradition of our monotheistic religious heritage asserts a meaningful order to the cosmos that facilitates our procreation and completion of the world.

It is, of course, always difficult to locate and then judge the significance of a cultural orientation, in this case optimism, as one of a number of factors contributing to liberty. Admittedly, it is methodologically a bit like grasping at air. It is much easier to focus on clearly tangible factors like promulgated law and institutional differentiation. Nonetheless, is it not the case that liberty requires an understanding of humanity's place in the cosmos that conveys hopefulness? If so, is it not also the case that liberty requires recognition of some kind of moral axis to the cosmos that provides a basis for that hopefulness? These are the problems before us posed by the *Atra-Ḫasīs*; for, as we have seen, the Mesopotamian account of the flood lacks any recognition of humanity's hopeful place in a meaningful order of the cosmos.

---

[14] Here, see Harold Berman, *Law and Revolution I: The Formation of the Western Legal Tradition* (Cambridge: Harvard University Press, 1985) and *Law and Revolution II: The Impact of the Protestant Reformations on the Western Legal Tradition* (Cambridge: Harvard University Press, 2003).

As a matter of fact, the *Atra-Ḥasīs* not only lacks an understanding of a meaningful order of the cosmos, it is an example of "classic polytheism" that, as such, explicitly conveys conceptual chaos. After the god Enki has told Atra-Ḥasīs of the approaching seven-day long flood, Atra-Ḥasīs, having assembled the city elders, conveys to them the following warning for what is about to occur,

"My god does not agree with your god,
Enki and Enlil are constantly angry with one another
… since I have always reverenced Enki, he told me this
…I can not set my feet on the earth of Enlil."[15]

With the assertion, "My god does not agree with your god, Enki and Enlil are constantly angry with one another," the reader is presented with an understanding of the cosmos as consisting of a continual conflict between forces that renders humanity psychologically hopeless, as even the human life of drudgery will presumably always be at risk of extinction, as it is subject to that conflict. Here, the reader finds humanity truly a pawn of an inscrutable, life-threatening, and life-denying fate against which no protest whatsoever is possible.[16] It is difficult to see how developed conceptions of liberty can exist within the pessimism of such a religious context.

"Classic polytheism" conveys this psychological pessimism, and, as we have observed, the *Atra-Ḥasīs* is a pristine example of it. One can't say quite the same for the Babylonian account of creation, the *Enuma Eliš*; for, there, the god of Babylon, Marduk, is portrayed as not only having become supreme within the Mesopotamian pantheon, but also, in its conclusion, as having incorporated within him the attributes (and even names) of the other fifty gods of the

---

[15] Foster, pp. 71-72, lines 38-44; Lambert and Millard, p. 91, lines 42-48.

[16] For a perceptive analysis of religious alternatives to this psychological pessimism, see Martin P. Nilsson, *Religion as Man's Protest Against the Meaninglessness of Events* (Lund: CWK Gleerup, 1954).

pantheon. Thus, the *Enuma Eliš* conveys an order to the cosmos created by Marduk—an account of creation and the deity that might be characterized as approaching "pagan monotheism."[17] The differences in this regard between the *Atra-Ḥasīs* and the *Enuma Eliš* deserve our careful attention, if for no other reason than as factors contributing to the clarification of the category "monotheism." Nevertheless, one gets the sense from the *Enuma Eliš* that whatever order does exist, it still provides no firm grounding for human freedom; for the cosmos remains an inhospitable environment for humanity. Whatever the order of the cosmos described in the *Enuma Eliš*, it provides no hopeful firmament for human psychology.

While we characterize the religion of the "great works" of ancient Greece as polytheist, for example, Aeschylus' *Oresteia* or *Prometheus Bound* or Euripides' *The Bacchae* or Hesiod's *Theogony*, those works are infused with a conception of justice, albeit differently so from one work to another, that is understood to be a part of Zeus, hence, the cosmos. This conceptual development also and obviously deserves our attention. This development is evidently not to be found in the *Atra-Ḥasīs*, making it, once again, a work worthy of the careful attention that we give to a "great work."[18] It may be that it richly warrants that attention as a means to explore the significance of the absence of hopefulness—and the reasons for that absence—in contrast to monotheism, but that is justification enough.

---

[17] For the category "pagan monotheism," see M.L. West, "Towards Monotheism" in Polymnia Athanassiadi and Michael Frede, *Pagan Monotheism in Late Antiquity* (Oxford: Oxford University Press, 1999), 21-40.

[18] This Mesopotamian pessimism is also to be observed in the Babylonian "Poem of a Righteous Sufferer," where the destruction and redemption of the sufferer are both attributed to Marduk, whose will, as a result, is inscrutable; and in the intriguing, so-called "Babylonian Theodicy" which seemingly concludes with the impression rejecting any cosmic justice or divine design. Both are found in Foster (1995).

## The Hebrew Bible

As we have briefly observed in the contrasts distinguishing the *Atra-Ḥasīs* from the Hebrew Bible, we are with the Hebrew Bible obviously entering into a different terrain made abundantly clear to the reader from the beginning, first chapter of Genesis: a meaningful order of the cosmos that provides a hopeful orientation to both our understanding of humanity and its activity. The problem that we encounter with the Hebrew Bible as a "great work" is whether or not it will be read on its own terms so that what it itself conveys may be properly understood.[19] Doing so requires that the two thousand year-old tradition of Christian exegesis of reading the Hebrew Bible as the Old Testament be suspended.

To avoid potential misunderstanding, I am not saying that this tradition of exegesis should be rejected. It is not the place for a scholar in the academic setting of a university to make such an argument. It is, however, appropriate for a scholar in a university setting to observe that suspending that tradition will better allow one to get to the text of the Hebrew Bible itself. However, encountering the Hebrew Bible on its own terms is not the only matter at stake here; for doing so will also clarify what is at stake in that tradition of exegesis. To refuse to proceed this way condemns the Hebrew Bible to being another neglected "great work" of the ancient Near East, irrespective of the attention paid to it.

One must be careful, under the pressure of a limited amount of time to devote to each work in an undergraduate course, not to confine examination of the Hebrew Bible to the opening chapters of Genesis, only to be followed by the presumed further development of

---

[19] For example, to appreciate properly the monotheism of the Hebrew Bible and specifically how to understand the plural pronouns in verses like Genesis 1:26 (see also Deuteronomy 32:8), attention should be paid to Psalm 82; see Peter Machinist, "How Gods Die, Biblically and Otherwise: A Problem of Cosmic Restructuring," in Beate Pongratz-Leisten, ed., *Reconsidering the Concept of Revolutionary Monotheism* (Winona Lake: Eisenbrauns, 2011), 189-240.

those chapters in the description of the suffering servant in Isaiah 52:13-53:12. This approach misrepresents the biblical material; specifically, there are four, not one, suffering servant songs in Isaiah, not just at 52:13-53:12 but also the earlier descriptions of the servant at Isaiah 42:1-4, 49:1-6, and 50:4-11. Thus, to understand properly the conceptually rich description of the servant in the fourth account, one ought to examine not only the fourth but actually the entire section from Isaiah, from chapter 42 through chapter 53. A careful reading requires that one proceed this way. Doing so will force upon the careful reader a number of otherwise well-known complications, such as the characterization of the Persian King, Cyrus, as the "messiah" (45:1) and the unambiguous identification of the servant as the collective Jacob/Israel at Isaiah 44:1 and 49:3. These are the kind of complications that ought to be taken into account in order to consider properly the interpretative difficulties of the famous description of the suffering servant in 52:13-53:12.

There is, however, a greater problem with indulging the temptation to approach the Hebrew Bible through the narrow lens of the opening chapters of Genesis and Isaiah 52-53. To proceed this way is to instill the incorrect impression that the orientation of the Hebrew Bible can be properly reduced to, or consists primarily of, a prophetic universalism. I don't deny that the latter is to be found in the Hebrew Bible. Nevertheless, to view the Hebrew Bible this way is to misrepresent it. To clarify the nature of this representation, consider, for example, one of its rarely examined laws.

> There shall be an area for you outside
> the camp, where you may relieve yourself.
> With your gear you shall have a spike, and
> when you have squatted you shall dig a hole with
> it and cover up your excrement.
>     (Deuteronomy 23:12-13)

Now, clearly the law of making and using a latrine has very little, if anything, to do with a prophetic universalism. It is difficult, to say the least, to imagine such an ordinance, even though of considerable importance, appearing in the New Testament. My intention in highlighting these verses from Deuteronomy is simply this: what this law indicates is the Hebrew Bible's manifest orientation to life in this world, and specifically to how that life should be organized to meet the requirements of living properly in this world.[20] Any approach to the Hebrew Bible that obscures in any way its orientation to the proper organization of life in this world woefully misrepresents it.

It is with this "this-worldly" orientation that a number of matters pertaining to the relation between religion and liberty arise. When I use the word "liberty," I do so with the meaning with which we usually use the term, that is, to be free from external coercion to engage at one's own initiative in activities, whether by oneself or in concert with others, and not as it is used in John 8:31-36 which refers to the coercion of sin. One clearly observes this understanding of liberty and its relation to the meaningful order of the cosmos in the description of the Israelite exodus from the Egyptian "house of slavery," where repeatedly we find the refrain of "Let my people go" (Exodus 5:1; 7:16; 8:1, 20; 9:1, 13; 10:3). However, it isn't merely a liberty expressed by the Israelites to be free from the coercion of Egyptian slavery, but a liberty for which the deity is described as being responsible. It is, thus, a liberty in accord with how things—the course of history and even the structure of the cosmos—should be. This manifest this-worldly conception of liberty, grounded in the order of the cosmos through recognition of the deity's specific act in history, is, in fact, only underscored by serving as the introduction to the Ten Commandments, "I am the LORD your God, who brought you out of the land of Egypt, out of the house of slavery" (Exodus 20:2, Deuteronomy 5:6). It is precisely because of the manifest orientation to this world that a number of well known problems of liberty unavoidably arise in the Hebrew Bible, for example, law, institutional differentiation, and the State.

---

[20] And so, for example, Deuteronomy 11:13-17.

Regarding the relation between law and liberty, we find in the Hebrew Bible the publically proclaimed "rule of law" necessary for liberty in contrast to the arbitrary rule of man, not only as described in Deuteronomy 17:14-20 (see also Joshua 24:25-27) but also as conveyed in several narratives, for example, the portrayal of Nathan's denunciation of King David (2 Samuel 12) or the theft of property in the episode of Naboth's vineyard (1 Kings 21). As has often been observed, Deuteronomy—including its covenantal structure and even its vocabulary—conveys equality before the law.[21] Regarding institutional differentiation and the qualification of otherwise unchecked power that it implies, we find the distinction between king and priest, including evidently between king and prophet such that no less than the prophesized future king from the House of David (1 Kings 13:2), Josiah, must turn to the prophetess Huldah to render authoritative judgment over the validity of a book of the law (2 Kings 22:11-20). Regarding the State, we apparently find recognition of the need for one in the literary complex beginning with Judges 17 and continuing to 1 Samuel 8.[22] Serving as the literary introduction to this complex is the verse "in those days there was no king in Israel; everyone did as he pleased" (Judges 17:1). Judges 18 begins with "In those days there was no king in Israel," only to be followed by the repetition of the same verse in Judges 19:1, as the introduction to the horrific description of how Israel had become Sodom. This description of Israel's descent into a morally anarchic hell concludes with the observation, "In those days there was no king in Israel; everyone did as he pleased" (Judges 21:25). The frequent repetition of these verses in these last five chapters of Judges surely indicates recognition of the need for a State, finally realized in the account of 1

---

[21] See, for example, Joshua Berman, "Egalitarian Politics: Constitution, Class, and the Book of Deuteronomy" in *Created Equal: How the Bible Broke with Ancient Political Philosophy* (Oxford: Oxford University Press, 2011), 51-80.

[22] On the thematic unity of this complex, see the form-critical study, Serge Frolov, *Judges* (Grand Rapids: Eerdmans, 2013).

Samuel 8-10. However, the rest of the history from that point through 2 Kings just as surely suggests the moral and political disaster from both having an over-bearing State and having an over-reliance on it.[23] These are, of course, all important matters, worthy of further, careful investigation, and especially so for the relation between religion and liberty. Nevertheless, as with the *Atra-Ḥasīs*, albeit as a negative exemplar, I wish to turn our attention to the all too easily overlooked psychological pre-conditions, conveyed in the Hebrew Bible, that seem to me to be necessary for liberty.

It is easy to be distracted by the details of the back-and-forth exchanges between Abraham and the deity in Genesis 18, as if the reader is having recounted the haggling over the price of an oriental rug in a Middle Eastern bazaar. Nevertheless, considerably more important in that exchange is the reason for it: whether or not the cosmos has a meaningful order to it so that an individual may have expectations that guide his or her behavior.

> Abraham came forward and said, "Will
> You sweep away the innocent along with the
> guilty? . . . Far be it from You to do
> such a thing, to bring death upon the innocent
> as well as the guilty, so that the innocent and guilty
> fare alike. Far be it from You! Shall not the Judge
> of all the earth deal justly?"
> (Genesis 18:23-25)

One observes in Abraham's questioning plea two recognitions: 1) that there is a distinction between innocent and guilty, and 2) an (anxious or anguished) expectation that this distinction matters to the deity, hence, to the order of the cosmos. At stake here is whether capriciousness or justice exists as fundamental to the order of the

---

[23] See, for example, Yoram Hazony, "The History of Israel, Genesis-Kings: A Political Philosophy" in *The Philosophy of Hebrew Scripture* (Cambridge: Cambridge University Press, 2012), 140-60.

cosmos, a justice that would also imply a necessary grounding for an ordered liberty. If there is no basis, we are plunged back into the conceptually chaotic and hopeless worldview of the Mesopotamian *Atra-Ḥasīs*.

The covenant in the Hebrew Bible is the conceptual vehicle for the recognition or assertion, as the case may be, of a meaningful order to the cosmos. In the first covenant, with Noah and his descendants, which, as such, is universal in its jurisdiction, one finds, once again, the prohibition against wanton murder—a prohibition, the justification for which is based upon the order of the cosmos: humanity is made in the image of God.[24] However, not to be overlooked is that the structure of the covenant is two-sided; for it not only conveys an expectation for proper human behavior, but also an expectation for the deity.[25] In the covenant with Noah, this second side of the covenant is the deity's promise to humanity,

> I will never again curse the ground because of humankind, for the inclination of the human heart is evil from youth; nor will I ever again destroy every living creature as I have done.

---

[24] The rabbis emphasized the universal jurisdiction of the so-called "Noahide code," expanding it to include seven laws; see Babylonian Talmud, Sanhedrin 56a-59a. This rabbinic interpretation of Genesis 9 entered into European political and juridical thought on natural law through Hugo Grotius, *The Rights of War and Peace* (1625) and John Selden's *De Iure Naturali & Gentium, Iuxta Disciplinam Ebraeorum* (1640).

[25] This two-sided expectation is true of the New Testament as well. It is true that the covenantal formulation of the New Testament conveys a perspective of selfless love, so, for example, Ephesians 2:4-10; John 3:16, 15:12-17; Matthew 6:3-4. However, the two-sided covenant of even this selfless love is apparent. So, for example, note the conclusion of Matthew 6:3-4, "But when you give alms, do not let your left hand know what your right hand is doing, so that your alms may be done in secret; *and your Father who sees in secret will reward you.*"

> I establish my covenant with you, that never again shall all flesh be cut off by the waters of a flood, and never again shall there be a flood to destroy the earth.
> (Genesis 8:21, 9:11; see also 9:15, 17)

This latter expectation of the deity—with, in the Hebrew Bible, its "practical", that is, its "this worldly" stance toward the conditions for life in this world—accounts for the heightened conceptual tension of Abraham's questions.

The pressing problem posed by Abraham's questions is what can humanity expect from the deity? The problem is not posed—it could not be posed—in the *Atra-Ḥasīs*. It is posed in the so-called "Babylonian Theodicy," but it could not be answered. Thus, these Mesopotamian "great works" were incapable of offering a secure basis for a hopeful stance toward the world. In contrast, the problem is both posed and answered throughout the Hebrew Bible. As we have seen, it is raised early on in Genesis by Abraham; its existence is taken for granted by the covenantal structure of Deuteronomy, specifically, the so-called "blessings and curses" in Deuteronomy 11:26-28 and Deuteronomy 27-30; Jeremiah confronts the problem in Jeremiah 12 and 15; and it is raised and answered again, albeit with profound complications, in Job.

It may very well be that the Hebrew Bible's orientation to life in this world can only result in intolerable frustrations of the hopeful expectations for humanity's existence in this world. That hope, integral to the covenantal relation between humanity and the deity in the Hebrew Bible, are the "this-worldly" expectations for descendants and the land necessary for their continued existence in this world, theologically further developed as the people chosen by God to dwell in the land promised to them: the "chosen people" and "promised land." These covenantal promises, made time and time again by the deity to Israel throughout the Hebrew Bible, represent an ontological obsession with life. This hopeful thirst for life is a pursuit of its quintessential expression, immortality; but the immortality being offered in the Hebrew Bible is, in contrast to the New Testament, confined to this world: the continued existence of Israel through its descendants. However, given the ceaseless tragedies of life that can only invite the possibility of the meaninglessness of human existence, Abraham's (and Job's) questions about the character of the deity, hence the cosmos, must arise. Furthermore, other problems of our existence, specifically, how life should be organized in this world—an examination that we call "politics" with its attendant problem of liberty—must also arise and be continually examined. Thus, the problems of law, institutions, and the State are not some kind of ancillary set of problems; rather, they must be seen as integral to the "this-worldly" orientation of the religion of the Hebrew Bible.

The profound difficulty in justifying and maintaining these hopeful expectations of life in the cosmos arise precisely because of the otherwise inexplicable vagaries of life—both for the individual (Job, Ecclesiastes) and historically for the polity (explicitly so in the entire literary complex of Joshua through 2 Kings), the historical expressions of which were the destruction of the northern kingdom of Israel by the Assyrians in 722 BCE and the destruction of the Temple by the Babylonians and exile in 586 BCE. True enough, the biblical authors recognized the tragic frustrations of their hopeful expectations and attempted to respond to them. An early response is seen in the re-evaluation of the covenantal relation in Amos 3:2.

> You alone have I singled out
> Of all the families of the earth—
> That is why I will call you to account
> For all your inquities.

This response to what might have otherwise been viewed as the hopelessness arising from the destruction of the northern kingdom of Israel by the Assyrians could not be laid at the feet of the deity; for to do so would have fractured conclusively the hope-bearing religion of Israel. Instead, the reason offered for the military and political destruction of the northern kingdom of the chosen people was their sinfulness. Thus, Assyria is understood as having become the rod of

God to punish the sinful Israelites (Isaiah 10:5). Nevertheless, a different religious logic could have been pursued: blaming God for the defeat of the chosen people. In fact, this alternative possibility was provocatively raised by the Judeans in the land of Egypt in the aftermath of the Babylonian destruction of Judah, as recounted in Jeremiah 44; but it was, of course, rejected by Jeremiah. Instead, as with Amos and Isaiah, the destruction is accounted for by the iniquities of the Israelites. The religious logic here is further extended by Jeremiah with his call for a new covenant, one that is revivified by faith, conveyed by the call to the Israelites to return to God by circumcising the foreskin of their hearts (Jeremiah 4:4; see also Deuteronomy 10:16, 30:6).[26]

Even these responses to the historical tragedies of Israel's historical existence maintain the context of the "this worldly" covenantal promises of descendants and land. Thus, in the continual re-examination of the nature of the deity, the cosmos, and political life that one finds in the Hebrew Bible, the centrality of the "this worldly" covenantal relation remains. However, in the effort to maintain that relation, heightened re-calibration of the character of the responsibility of humanity for its actions in the completion of creation of this world takes place, placing psychologically acute burdens on the individual, as one can observe with Jeremiah's self-conscious autobiographical reflections. Precisely therein lies one avenue of the Hebrew Bible's hopefulness, however tenuous it may be in the face of the treacherous events of history. The acute conceptual tensions that arise in the attempt to provide a hope-bearing meaning to those hope-destroying historical events may have been alleviated by a messianic historical outlook; but given the continuing focus on this world, they could not be eliminated within the framework of the Hebrew Bible.

---

[26] The obvious oddness of the metaphor leads one inescapably to the conclusion that it must be an intra-biblical commentary on the circumcision of the foreskin of the penis (Genesis 17:10-12, Joshua 5:2-7).

## Conclusion

It is highly probable that for any and all civilizations there has always existed some kind of idea of liberty. After all, surely anyone at any time and everywhere resents being ordered what to do, and all the more so when the authoritarian command utterly disregards, let alone undermines, one's perceived interests, resulting in, for example, the burden of excessive taxation, crushing debt, and, of course, slavery. Thus, it should not be surprising that we do not have to turn first to ancient Greece for evidence of the existence of concepts of freedom. We find various terms throughout the approximately three thousand year-long history of Mesopotamian civilization that expressed an idea of liberty, specifically, the Sumerian term *amargi* (*amagi*) and the Akkadian terms *andurāru* and *zakûtu*.[27] Given the purpose of this paper as a call for programs of the "great works" or "great ideas" to cease neglecting the literature of the ancient Near East, I shall not enter into a detailed examination of the complications of those terms. It will suffice here merely to note those terms; and to observe further that all three, while conveying a meaning of liberty, do so in the sense of a return to an earlier or original state, hence relating to manumission of slaves or escaping from forced labor (with its associated "asylum") and relief from or remission of taxes and debt, all of which would re-establish the individual to a condition before he or she was a slave or subjected to forced labor or enduring the burden of excessive taxation.[28]

---

[27] For the Akkadian terms *andurāru* and *zakûtu*, see the *Chicago Assyrian Dictionary*; and Daniel C. Snell, *Flight and Freedom in the Ancient Near East* (Leiden: Brill, 2001), especially chapter one, "The History of Freedom and Getting Away," 11-30, and Snell's bibliography. The logo for the American foundation Liberty Fund is the cuneiform for *amagi*, http://www.libertyfund.org/logo.html.

[28] Regarding the return to an original state, note that the etymology for *amargi* is "returning to the mother." The etymology for *andurāru* is likely *durāru*, meaning "turning" or "returning."

We find an example of the use of *andurāru*, as signifying freedom in the sense of a return to an earlier or original state, in the *Atra-Ḫasīs* in its description of the creation of humanity to relieve the Igigi-gods of the labor imposed upon them by the other, greater gods.

> I [Mami, the birth goddess] have done away with your [the Iggi-gods] heavy forced labor.
> I have imposed your drudgery on man.
> You have bestowed clamor upon mankind.
> I have released the yoke, I have established [your] freedom [*andurā*[*ra*], literally, "I have made restoration"].[29]

It would appear that while these terms do express an idea of freedom, their meaning revolves primarily around the lifting of an imposed burden (taxation, forced labor, and so forth), thereby restoring one to a state before the burden was imposed. Perhaps this sense of freedom is captured by our use of the word "liberate," as in to free one from a burden, rather than the liberty to do something different or new as one pleases. Thus, it does not seem to convey a meaning of freedom where one is free to pursue an activity entirely at one's own initiative, that is, a meaning of freedom that assumes a hopeful psychological openness to the world that, in turn, is yours to fashion.

If this understanding of the Mesopotamian conception of freedom as referring to the restoration of an earlier or original condition is correct, one would like to know why this conception did not undergo further development. What accounts for what seems to be obstacles to the generalization of the idea? We certainly find in numerous works from Mesopotamian literature complaints against injustice. In perhaps the most famous example, one that is sometimes read as a "great work," *The Epic of Gilgamesh*, one observes the pressing lament of the people of Uruk for justice in its opening

---

[29] Foster, p. 59, lines 231-34; Lambert and Millard, pp. 59-61, lines 240-43.

description of the arrogant authoritarianism, including the tyranny of a sexual predator, of Gilgamesh. And in a work that is not read as a "great work," the so-called Cyrus Cylinder, we find that Cyrus "returned the images of the gods [of the previously conquered peoples] to their places and let them dwell in their eternal abodes."[30] Nevertheless, the problem still remains; for we find no generalization of the conception of freedom; and it is certainly not justified to think that Cyrus' edict was based upon any kind of developed conception of religious liberty.

There must be numerous reasons for why this conceptual generalization did not take place. Once again, the absence of developed legal codes about private property and institutional differentiation surely were factors. However, this set of factors only begs the question; for why didn't those more tangible factors and their attendant social relations that would have facilitated the generalization of the idea of freedom arise in Mesopotamian history?

These are worthy problems to be taken up in programs devoted to the "great works" or "great ideas." In responding to these problems, can one avoid the conclusion that the fertile cultural assumptions that would have allowed for the further development of the conception of liberty were absent? Here, we enter into the domain of ideas: how one idea may influence another. Underlying the possibility of such an influence is the question of the extent to which there is a unitary (but not uniform) orientation of a culture expressing that domain of ideas: in the context of these remarks, a pessimistic Mesopotamian culture and an optimistic ancient Israelite culture.[31] If we are justified to enter into this domain in pursuit of answers to the questions posed above, can one avoid observing that the conceptual chaos of polytheism was

---

[30] For the biblical understanding of Cyrus' edict, see Ezra 1:1-4, 5:13-17, 6:1-15, 7:11-26, and 2 Chronicles 36:22-23.

[31] The problem here is heuristic, that is, is it not only possible but also helpful to characterize a culture by a primary orientation? While it may be possible to describe an orientation as primary or "unitary," numerous conceptual tensions within the culture would still exist, and that is why it should not be understood as "uniform."

one such cultural factor that either contributed to, or was expressive of, the obstacle to the further development of the conception of liberty? While the Mesopotamian individual, qua individual, surely had an idea of his or her future, and just as surely had hope for a better future, that hopefulness was circumscribed or frustrated by that Mesopotamian pessimistic cultural chaos captured so succinctly by Atra-Ḫasīs' statement, "my god does not agree with your god."

The merit of this line of deliberation is to revive what is currently no longer a fashionable assumption, namely, that the religion of a society is the vehicle for, or expressive of, the orientation of a culture. As such, religion must have had a bearing on the development of a conception of liberty (and vice-versa). Thus, the lack of a further rationalization of the conceptual world of religion would find its counterpart in the lack of a conceptual generalization of the conception of freedom. One need not assume some kind of teleology at work in the process of the rationalization of religion and the generalization of the conception of freedom. The rationalization of religion leading from polytheism to monotheism suppressed but could not eliminate previous conceptual difficulties, for example, whether or not there is a meaningful order to the cosmos, and the extent to which that order provides a basis for hopefulness that would, in turn, foster a conceptual environment for the further development of the idea of liberty. That these conceptual difficulties could not be eliminated is only one more reason for not neglecting the "great works" of the ancient Near East.

2

# FACTION AGAINST FACTION
## EMPEROR JULIAN ON RELIGIOUS TOLERANCE

*Jeremiah H. Russell*

Tolerance is a self-evident good in Western liberal democracies. No justification is required. As a matter of fact, intolerance is one of our culture's gravest sins. Yet such self-evidence was not always the case. Granted, every culture displays some degree of tolerance; no society can be intolerant of everything, but tolerance, especially religious tolerance, required apologists.[1] And it seems those calls for tolerance were loudest in the early modern period. With the fracturing of Christendom via the Protestant Reformation and the rise of the nation-state, intolerance reached a heightened status (e.g., Thirty Year's War, 1618-1648). These apologists argued tolerance was good for the welfare of the regime. It quelled civil unrest and promoted the well-being of the citizenry. What is more, they said, it was good for religion itself. Inasmuch as religious tolerance offered some free exercise, it protected faith traditions from state corruption and allowed citizens to worship without violating their conscience. By and large, these justifications persuaded those in the West to tolerate

---

[1] For philosophical arguments for tolerance, see John Locke, *Letter Concerning Toleration*; Voltaire, *A Treatise on Toleration*; James Madison, *Memorial and Remonstrance against Religious Assessments*; Thomas Jefferson, "Letter to the Danbury Baptists" and *Notes on the State of Virginia*; and John Stuart Mill, "Of the Liberty of Thought and Discussion," in *On Liberty*. For theological arguments for tolerance, see Tertullian, *To Scapula*; Lactantius, *Divine Institutes*; John Milton, *Aeropagetica*; John Owen, "Indulgence and Toleration Considered;" and Roger Williams, *The Bloudy Tenet, of Persecution, for Cause of Conscience*.

religious differences, and these very justifications are used today—it is good for the state, and it is good for religion.

However, tolerance was not always used for such altruistic ends, particularly in regards to religion. Perhaps the first to offer expansive religious tolerance[2] after Christianity rose to political prominence was one of the most noted antagonists of the faith—the Emperor Julian, otherwise known as the Apostate (331-363).[3] From the earliest days of his brief reign, he appeared tolerant. He permitted every religious sect to worship freely and made it clear that no religious violence, either by Christians or pagans, would be condoned.[4] He summoned Christian bishops to the imperial palace and exhorted them to "lay aside their differences and allow every man to practice his belief boldly without hindrance," and to his fellow pagans, he said, "we ought to persuade and instruct men, not by blows or insults, or bodily violence."[5] Here, the emperor appears ahead of this time, yet I argue that, though he appears benevolent on the surface, his tolerance did not originate from a desire to protect faith traditions from state

---

[2] I use the term "tolerance" as opposed to "liberty" in part because the former carries a negative connotation consistent with Julian's attitude toward Christianity.

[3] To be sure, Emperors Constantine and Licinius come to mind as tolerant predecessors. After all, it was they who ended Christian persecution and issued the Edict of Milan. Yet, within a few years of the edict, Licinius restored persecution, and Constantine ostracized various Christian sects, including some later deemed orthodox. Regarding Constantine's policies on religious tolerance, see H.A. Drake, *Constantine and the Bishops: The Politics of Intolerance* (Baltimore, MD: Johns Hopkins University Press, 2000) and Elizabeth Digeser, *The Making of a Christian Empire: Lactantius and Rome* (Ithaca, NY: Cornell University Press, 2000).

[4] Julian, "Letter to the Citizens of Bostra," in *The Works of the Emperor Julian*, vol. 3, trans. by W.C. Wright (Cambridge, MA: Harvard University Press, 1923), 436a. See "Letter to Atarbius," 376c-d.

[5] Ammianus Marcellinus, *The Later Roman Empire*, 22.5. See Julian, "Letter to Atarbius," "Letter to Hecebolius," and "Letter to the Citizens of Bostra," in *The Works of Emperor Julian*, vol. 3, trans. by W.C. Wright (Cambridge, MA: Harvard University Press, 1923).

corruption or allow citizens to worship without violating their conscience, as modern apologists argued. Rather, he used tolerance as a mechanism to neutralize, if not subvert, Christianity by pitting the various factions within the faith against one another.[6]

## The Apostate and the Faith

In order to make a persuasive case about Julian's use of religious tolerance, it is important to understand his overall disposition toward Christianity. If people know anything about him, it is more than likely his apostasy from the faith. He was the nephew of Emperor Constantine, was baptized and catechized as a Christian, but had a religious "conversion"[7] to paganism at age twenty, a conversion he kept quiet until his rise to Augustus. For the Apostate, Christianity was politically troublesome. It "overturned almost everything"[8] and brought disorder to the empire. During his brief reign, he attempted to "cleanse away all impiety"[9] and cure Rome of this "disease." In Julian's eyes, there were three political problems with the faith: its alleged universality, its allegiance to an authority above the regime, and its apparent weak and slave ethic.

---

[6] Many scholars argue to the contrary. For example, one of the most definitive intellectual biographers of the emperor suggests that he actually was benevolent early in his reign but took subversive measures later. See Joseph Bidez, *La vie de l'empereur Julien*, (Paris, 1930), 261-65, 310-14.

[7] By conversion, I mean A.D. Nock's famous formulation, which includes a change in belief, an exclusive adherence to those beliefs, and a strong repugnance of one's former way of life (*Conversion: The Old and the New in Religion from Alexander the Great to Augustine of Hippo* [Oxford University Press, 1933]). Most scholars accept Julian's conversion in this sense of the word, yet some argue he never converted because he never was Christian. See Polymnia Athanassiadi, *Julian: An Intellectual Biography* (New York, NY: Oxford University Press, 1981), 24-27.

[8] Julian, "Letter to Atarbius."

[9] Julian, *Letter to the Cynic Heraclius*, in *The Works of Emperor Julian*, vol. 2, trans. by W.C. Wright (Cambridge, MA: Harvard University Press, 1913), 231d.

The first political problem was Christianity's alleged universality. With his uncle Constantine's victory over Maxentius, some argued the Christian God was vindicated as the true universal monarch, particularly over and against the pagan deity, Sol Invictus.[10] However, Julian disagreed: Christianity's claim to universality was invalid in part because of a theological error. In short, Christians mistook the particular deity of the Israelites—the God of Abraham, Isaac, and Jacob—for the truly universal God. For Julian, the Christian God was simply one of the many lower, particular gods of the Roman pantheon. As a matter of fact, he refused to call Christianity by its given name. He referred to the faithful as "Galileans" and described Jesus as "the Nazarene" to emphasize their particularity. Hence, as emperor, Julian sought to curb the spread of Christianity and to restore Roman paganism, which he believed was truly universal and thus solely sufficient for the civil religion of a universal Empire.

This mistaken claim to universality proved politically problematic, Julian argued, because it was too exclusive. Or to state it more politically, it was too particular to support the Roman *oikoumene*. On several occasions throughout his corpus, Julian referred to Christianity as "atheism." To modern hearers, this label sounds strange, but it was a common charge made by Romans against the faith. The most illuminating reference is found in *Against the Galileans*.[11] Here, he described the new religion as an amalgam of two variant traditions—Hellenism and Judaism. "From both religions," he writes, "they have gathered what has been engrafted like powers of evil, as it were, on these nations—atheism from the Jewish levity, and a sordid and slovenly way of living from our [Hellenic] indolence and vulgarity."

---

[10] See for example Eusebius, *Ecclesiastical History, Preparation for the Gospel*, and *In Praise of Constantine*.

[11] In *The Works of Emperor Julian*, vol. 3, trans. by W.C. Wright (Cambridge, MA: Harvard University Press, 1923), 43a-b. See also "Letter to a Priest," in *The Works of Emperor Julian*, vol. 2, trans. by W.C. Wright (Cambridge, MA: Harvard University Press, 1913), 305d, and "Misopogon," in *The Works of Emperor Julian*, vol. 2, trans. by W.C. Wright (Cambridge, MA: Harvard University Press, 1913), 357d.

Though he did not elaborate on the term here, he restated the thesis in another fragment, which clarifies the ambiguity.[12] From the Jews, Julian argues, Christians adopted monotheism. As a matter of fact, he says this was the only thing they adopted from their Hebraic forefathers. But in what sense is monotheism atheism? Of course, Christianity (and Judaism for that matter) was not atheistic in the traditional sense; still, it dismissed the hundreds of pagan deities worshipped in Roman religion. In the Hebrew Scriptures for example, the Israelites were forbidden from serving all the gods save only the God of Abraham, Isaac, and Jacob.[13] This Christian "atheism" was too particular to support the Roman *oikoumene* because it denied, or even viewed as demonic, those deities that were traditionally considered the source of imperial laws and customs.

Another political problem for Julian was the Christian allegiance to an authority above the regime. In his mind, Christians had little respect for law. "You have thought it a slight thing to diminish and to add to the things which were written in the law," he writes, "and to transgress it completely you have thought to be in every way more manly and high-spirited."[14] Granted, the law in question is the Mosaic Law, which one might consider religious, not political. Still, a sharp distinction between the religious and the political was not as clear in antiquity, if it existed at all, and what is more, it still indicates a dismissive disposition toward law. Julian contrasted the Christian disposition with their Hellenic and Hebraic counterparts. The Hellenes follow the traditions of their forefathers, he argues, and the Jews honor precise laws concerning religious worship and observances; they "are so ardent in their belief that they would choose to die for it, and to endure utter want and starvation rather than taste pork or any animal that has been strangled or had the life squeezed

---

[12] Julian, *Against the Galileans*, 238b.
[13] Julian cites Deuteronomy 32:9.
[14] Julian, *Against the Galileans*, 320b-c.

out of it."[15] Whether Jews were as devoted as he claims or whether he exaggerated for rhetorical effect, it is clear that he praised their dedication to the law. Christians, by contrast, eat everything "even as the green herb," an apparent mantra alluding to their freedom from Jewish dietary laws.[16]

The emperor discussed several examples of their disregard for Mosaic Law. These were disconcerting because, viewed as a radical sect of Judaism, Christians were neglecting their own religious duties. One such example was their lack of animal sacrifice.[17] (It is no surprise he mentioned this because it was a vital component in pagan religion and one aspect of Judaism he actually praised.) Animal sacrifice was fundamental to biblical Judaism. Abraham built altars to God and sacrificed continually, as the Hellenes did. Moses later established various methods of sacrifice: both sacrifices of atonement and of purification. The prophet even commanded that the feast of Passover, which included a sacrificial lamb, be kept forever.[18] Yet a major problem arose in the first century AD—Roman legions, under the leadership of Titus, overtook Jerusalem and destroyed the Temple, the place at least historically where sacrifices were performed. Naturally, Christians argued that Jews could no longer sacrifice; they disregarded these laws out of necessity. But even apart from the loss of the Temple, Julian argues, Christians did not sacrifice for they had a "new kind of sacrifice." It is unclear whether he was referring to the historical death of Jesus or the sacrifice of the Mass. Either he was saying Christians thought they no longer needed to sacrifice because of Jesus' death, or the sacrifice of the Mass was not a

---

[15] Julian, "Letter to Theodorus," in *The Works of Emperor Julian*, vol. 3, trans. by W.C. Wright (Cambridge, MA: Harvard University Press, 1923), 453c-d.

[16] This phrase is part of Genesis 9:3, which reads "[a]ny living creature that moves about shall be yours to eat; I give them all to you even as the green herb." It suggests the freedom to eat any living thing, though the following verse prohibits eating the blood of any animal.

[17] Julian, *Against the Galileans*, 305d-306b, 343c-343d, 354b-356e.

[18] Exodus 12:14-15.

real sacrifice in the traditional sense, that is an animal sacrifice as practiced in both Hellenism and Judaism. Either way, for him, they neglected the law.

Christians had such low regard for these and other laws, in Julian's estimation, because their allegiance to apostolic authority trumped their obligation to law.[19] Take the dietary laws for example. Christians felt no obligation to these laws because of Peter's vision. In bewilderment, Julian asks, "Why are we so ready to believe him [Peter] in such important matters? Was it so hard a thing that Moses enjoined on you when, besides the flesh of swine, he forbade you to eat winged things and things that dwell in the sea, and declared to you that besides the flesh of swine these also had been cast out by God and shown to be impure?"[20] These laws were maintained by the Jewish people for hundreds of years, yet they were quickly pushed aside because one man heard a voice (i.e., apostolic authority). Julian saw a serious political problem with apostolic authority—it held more weight with Christians than the law itself. Thus, a believer, who could disregard a law given by their own God upon permission of an apostle, would have little hesitation in disregarding a law propagated by man.[21]

---

[19] Christians offered other justifications for their abandonment of the Mosaic Law. For instance, they argued it was only intended as a temporary custodian. The emperor attempted to demonstrate the contrary, namely that the law was eternally binding. Though he does not offer the "ten thousand passages" promised, he cites several, only one of which survives in the fragments: "And this day shall be unto you for a memorial; and you shall keep it a feast to the Lord throughout your generations; you shall keep it a feast by an ordinance forever" (Ex. 12:14-15). This reference to the requirements and procedures of Passover was abrogated by Jesus' death, Christians argued, even though the memorial is explicitly established forever in the passage.

[20] Julian, *Against the Galileans*, 314d-e.

[21] Such freedom is consistent with the citizens Julian encountered in Antioch, who could not bear "even to hear the name of slavery, whether it be slavery to the gods or the laws. For sweet is liberty in all things!" (*Misopogon*, 343b-c). Julian argued that the citizens of Antioch made Jesus their

A third, and final, problem was the type of citizen Christianity produced. Julian was forced to address this concern because of Christianity's growing influence in the Empire, and he was highly critical of its influence because he believed the religion lacked the vitality of paganism. Rome's greatness, in his eyes, was due to Hellenism.[22] Christians, he thought, embodied the slavish *ethos* of their Jewish forefathers. The Jews were a race of slaves. Abraham was an alien in a foreign land; Jacob, a slave to many nations. Granted, Moses freed his people, who were in captivity for roughly four centuries, but after being released and wandering in the desert for decades, they were still subject to judges and slaves to foreign races, and though the emperor acknowledged they had a kingdom, he belittled it in part because of its brief existence.

The Jews were slaves, the emperor argued, because they did not possess the virtues requisite for civilization. They lacked the courage and military expertise needed to sustain and to defend an empire's vast territory. In Julian's eyes, no Jew could compare to Julius Caesar or Alexander the Great; the closest perhaps were Samson and David. Samson was known for his strength.[23] As a young man, he reportedly wrestled a lion with his bare hands, and in a rage, single-handedly slaughtered thirty Philistines. After this and other exploits, the Philistines demanded his detainment, but in the process, he broke free, grabbed the jawbone of a donkey, and slaughtered one-thousand Philistines. David's fame began with the slaughter of another Philistine, Goliath.[24] As commander of the Israelite army, he brought two hundred foreskins (twice as many as requested) to the king in order to win his daughter's hand in marriage. Later as king, David brought stability to the region, united the tribes of Israel, conquered

---

"guardian," whom they believed justified their freedom from the law (357b-c).

[22] Julian, *Against the Galileans*, 106b-e, 176a-c, 178b, 184b-c, 190c, 193c-d, 194b-d, 201e-202a, 209d-210a, 213a-c, 218a-c.

[23] The life of Samson is recorded in the book of Judges 13-16.

[24] For an account of the life of David, see 1 Samuel 17-31, 2 Samuel 1-24, and 1 Chronicles 10-29.

the city of Jerusalem, and vanquished the remaining Canaanites. Yet according to Cyril of Alexandria, in a lost fragment, Julian demeaned these accomplishments, questioned their courage, and pointed out their limited dominion.[25]

As far as Julian was concerned, Jesus only continued his forefathers' slavishness. The Nazarene was of humble origins—the son of a carpenter, born in a lowly manger, and a subject of Caesar. Even his public ministry, the emperor argued, was anything but noble. "Jesus, who won over the least worthy of you, has been known by name for but little more than three hundred years," he writes, "and during his lifetime he accomplished nothing worth hearing of, unless anyone thinks that to heal crooked and blind men and to exorcise those possessed by evil demons…can be classified as a mighty achievement."[26] Such was illustrated by the fact that Jesus was not mentioned by the historians of his day.[27] Reminiscent of an adage attributed to Pliny the Elder that "true glory consists in doing what deserves to be written," the Apostate suggested that Jesus was not great because his acts were unfit for immortality. Perhaps, if Christianity was not as public and politically influential as it was in the fourth century, Julian would have paid it no attention, but it was

---

[25] Julian, *Against the Galileans*, 176c, n.5.

[26] Ibid., 191d-e. Interestingly, he proposed the Greek god, Asclepius, as an alternative to Jesus. This deity, who Julian said was the "savior of all men," was charged with healing the sick. It is unclear what made Asclepius' work worthy of immortality and Jesus' undeserving.

[27] The two earliest references to Jesus appear to be Jewish historian Josephus (*Antiquities*, 20.9.1) and the Roman historian Tacitus (*Annals*, 15.44). The first mention of Christianity by a Roman is in a letter written to Emperor Trajan from Pliny the Younger. He called Christianity a "club" (*hetaerias*), which was a social or political association often viewed with suspicion for they sometimes served as venues for political dissension. Celsus, *The True Doctrine* (177 AD), and Porphyry, *Against the Christians* (third century), are the two earliest polemics against Christianity.

this increasing influence that concerned him.[28] If Romans imitated Jesus, instead of their Hellenic forefathers, if they instituted the wisdom of the Nazarene, he believed Rome would be undone: "Listen to a fine statesmanlike piece of advice," he sneers, "'Sell [all] that you have to the poor….' Can anyone praise this teaching, when if it be carried out, no city, no nation…will hold together."[29]

For these three fundamental reasons, Julian took political measures to neutralize Christianity. He reversed the faith's privileged status given by Constantine and his successor.[30] He removed the clergy's exemption status from political service in the Senate. He revoked their privilege to use the imperial courier system (*cursus publicus*), a publicly funded travel system used for government business. He issued an edict forbidding day-time burial rites, a Christian practice considered abominable to pagans, and perhaps most famous of all, he issued an edict forbidding Christians from teaching philosophy, poetry, or rhetoric in the academies, an edict that his ardent defender, Ammianus Marcellinus, described as a "harsh act which should be buried in lasting oblivion."[31]

## Instances of Religious Tolerance

Seemingly in contrast with this disposition toward Christianity, Julian offered tolerance to its followers. This policy is best illustrated by two specific examples, namely amnesty for Christians exiled under previous emperors and an attempted restoration of the Jewish Temple in Jerusalem. (It might seem strange to include this second example,

---

[28] The emperor argued that Jesus and the apostles (or at least Paul) never intended to be as public or politically influential as later ecclesiastical leadership. They (Jesus and Paul) were "content to delude maidservants and slaves," he writes (*Against the Galileans*, 206a).

[29] Julian, "Fragment 5," in *The Works of Emperor Julian*, vol. 3, trans. by W.C. Wright (Cambridge, MA: Harvard University Press, 1923).

[30] See *Codex Theodosianus* 12.1.50.

[31] Ammianus Marcellinus, *The Later Roman Empire*, 22.10.

but for Julian, Christianity was a radical sect of Judaism, and thus the Restoration would have been related in his mind.)

## Return of the Exiles

Julian became emperor during the most threatening theological controversy Christianity had yet encountered. A controversy over the nature of Jesus arose in Alexandria between the bishop, Alexander, and an influential presbyter, Arius. The bishop took the position that the Son was coeternal with the Father and was not created; Arius, the position that he was not coeternal and thus created. "There was a time when the Son was not," Arians argued. Alexander removed Arius from his post, but some bishops from around the eastern part of the empire supported Arius and accused Alexander of heresy. The controversy soon threatened to divide the church, especially in the East. In 325, Emperor Constantine called an ecumenical council at Nicaea in hopes of settling the issue. Though the council took an anti-Arian position, proclaiming that the Son was one in being (*homoousios*) with the Father, the controversy was not over. To be sure, Constantine deposed those who disagreed with the creed, including Arius, but was soon persuaded by Eusebius of Nicomedia (who later baptized the emperor) to restore the excommunicated. Not only were the Arians restored, they started to receive imperial favors, including the exile of orthodox clergy.

Soon after becoming Augustus,[32] Julian did something rather strange—he offered amnesty to all previously exiled Christians. The reason for this is never explicitly declared by the emperor, but it should be clear that amnesty was not given because he wanted the faith to flourish. It was a "disease" responsible in large part for bringing disorder to the empire. It should also be clear he did not offer amnesty to the exiles, mostly orthodox, because he favored their

---

[32] Some argue that the actual edict was issued earlier, while Julian was merely Caesar. See Timothy Barnes, *Athanasius and Constantius: Theology and Politics in the Constantinian Empire*, (Cambridge, MA: Harvard University Press, 2001), 154-55.

theological position. As a matter of fact, he seemed more sympathetic to the Arian doctrine. He abhorred the idea that a deity could be "born of the flesh." This is suggested in a letter often read as a sort of preface to *Against the Galileans*.[33] Here, he stated that one of the Christian doctrines that particularly upset him was the position that Jesus, the divine Son, was born of the Virgin Mary. In another text, the emperor allegorized a pagan myth regarding the birth of Dionysus in order to avoid a similar interpretation.[34] According to the story, Dionysus was a son of Zeus, born of a mortal named Semele, yet the emperor suggested the reader set aside "all this nonsense" and get to the truth of the matter, which was that Semele should be considered his "mother" in the sense that she foretold his earthly manifestation, not that she literally gave birth to a god.

The reason Julian offered amnesty, I suggest, is actually alluded to by Ammianus Marcellinus: "as this freedom increased their [Christians'] dissension, he might afterwards have no fear of a united populace, knowing as he did from experience that no wild beasts are such enemies to mankind as are most of the Christians in their deadly hatred of one another."[35] The historian proposed that Julian's

---

[33] The letter was addressed to another Christian bishop, Photinus, who adhered to a Christology neither Arian nor orthodox. R.P.C. Hanson calls it a type of "middle Marcellism," i.e., a doctrine influenced by the teachings of Marcellus, who was accused of non-trinitarianism (*The Search for the Christian Doctrine of God: The Arian Controversy, 318-81* [Grand Rapids, MI: Baker, 2006]). For ancient sources discussing Photinus, see Socrates Scholasticus, *Ecclesiastical History*, 2.18-19 and Sozomen, *Ecclesiastical History*, 4.6.

[34] Julian, *Letter to the Cynic Heraclius*, in *The Works of the Emperor Julian*, vol. 2, trans. by W.C. Wright (Cambridge, MA: Harvard University Press, 1913), 220b-222c.

[35] Trans. by John Rolfe (Cambridge, MA: Harvard University Press, 1935), 22.5.4. Some Christians had similar interpretations. For example, Philostorgius writes, "He contrived to bring into open collision the bishops who had been banished for various reasons and those who had been substituted in their room. Accordingly he gave to both parties full licence of

tolerance toward the religious, which certainly included his amnesty toward the exiled, was offered in hopes of undermining the faith.

In some cases, Julian's amnesty had the destructive effect Ammianus suggested. Perhaps the clearest example was in Antioch.[36] Christians there were already divided prior to Julian's ascension to power. Antioch was a center of Nicene orthodoxy under bishop Eustathius, yet he was deposed in 330 due to false sexual allegations most likely made by Arian dissidents. At this time, Constantius was emperor, and Arians knew they had his ear. Under his protection, Arians took over ecclesiastical leadership, but a minority sect still faithful to Eustathius worshipped separately. After an Arian bishop left Antioch for Constantinople in 360, Meletius was appointed. He was quickly exiled (less than one month after election).[37] He was replaced by Euzoius, an Arian, who had the emperor's sympathy. During the reign of Constantius, there were two sects in Antioch—the majority Arian sect and a minority faction committed to Eustathius and Nicene orthodoxy. Yet Julian further complicated religious life in Antioch by issuing amnesty. Meletius returned to Antioch and attempted to reclaim his role as bishop. Naturally, the Arian sect remained faithful to Euzoius, and the orthodox faction, not loyal to Meletius the first time, was not loyal this time either. Yet, there was a small sect of Christians who aligned with the recent exile.

---

doing whatever they could to obtain their restoration and to defend their possessions respectively" (*Ecclesiastical History*, 8.4).

[36] Theodoret used this same example to illustrate the schism cultivated by Julian. See *Ecclesiastical History*, 3.2. For literature on the schism in Antioch, see Barnes, *Athanasius and Constantius*, 155-56; Hanson, *The Search for the Christian Doctrine of God*, 509, 643-44; Wendy Mayer and Pauline Allen, *The Churches of Syrian Antioch (300-638 CE)* (Peeters, 2012); Glanville Downey, *A History of Antioch in Syria: From Seleucus to the Arab Conquest* (Princeton University Press, 1961); Christine Shepardson, *Controlling Contested Places: Late Antique Antioch and the Spatial Politics of Religious Controversy* (Berkeley, CA: University of California Press, 2014).

[37] For the controversy regarding his exile, see Thomas Karmann, *Meletius von Antiochien* (Peter Lang, 2009), 135-149.

During Julian's reign, there were three factions within the city—the Arians faithful to the bishop Euzoius, those who accepted the authority of Meletius, and those faithful to Eustathius. The schism was so deep it took over fifty years before Christians in Antioch recognized a single bishop.

His subversive intentions, however, were most manifest when the tactic failed, especially in the case of Athanasius of Alexandria, one of the most controversial and yet influential theologians of the fourth century. Thus Julian's decision to return clergy to their posts, particularly Athanasius, made sense. Most exiles were part of the minority sect, and there was perhaps no better candidate to stir up turmoil than Athanasius. This "common little man"[38] as Julian called him was exiled on five different occasions by four different emperors. In 335, Constantine banished this bishop to Tyre for period of over two years in part because of his reputation for disturbing the peace. Julian permitted his return from exile under Constantius, and Athanasius returned to Egypt as bishop but did not spark the same divisiveness that Meletius did. Actually, he did the opposite. He worked to unite the orthodox factions of Christianity and even addressed the conflict in Antioch that deepened when Meletius returned. Almost immediately after his exile, Athanasius presided over a regional council, and one of the documents from that council, *Tomus ad Antiochenos*, attempted to persuade the two orthodox factions in Antioch to reconcile.[39] There were calls throughout the letter for concord. The council asked those under Meletius to recognize the authority of the bishop presiding over those faithful to Eustathius and ordered that no belief beyond the Nicene doctrine was required. Even though the council's attempt at unification failed, the emperor was still troubled by Athanasius' actions. He quickly sent a letter to the citizens expressing his dissatisfaction. He accused the

---

[38] This is most likely the origin of Athanasius' rather famous nickname "the black dwarf."

[39] See also *Epistula Catholica*. Though most scholars consider the document spurious, it contains similar themes of unity.

bishop of violating the law, which Julian rather conveniently interpreted as permission only to return to his native land, not his role in the church.[40] There is no indication that this was Julian's original intent, and if it was, it is odd that there is no record of such dissatisfaction regarding Meletius' reappointment. Regardless, the emperor ordered Athanasius to leave Alexandria. The bishop complied. He stayed in Egypt and continued to influence Christians there. Julian's true intention regarding amnesty is then revealed. The emperor wrote a letter to Ecdicius, prefect of Egypt, demanding his expulsion from the entire region, even though the citizens of Alexandria petitioned for him to return.[41] The Apostate expressed disappointment that the Egyptians were duped by such a "clever rascal" and a "contemptible puppet" as Athanasius and in anger added "I only wish that, along with Athanasius, the wickedness of his impious school had been suppressed."[42] In his rage, his true intention slipped—he wanted Athanasius and his sect suppressed. The emperor used subversive tactics to accomplish this goal, but they backfired.

## Rebuild the Temple

A second example of Julian's tolerance (or one could even say promotion) of the faith from which Christianity sprang was his attempt to rebuild the Jewish Temple in Jerusalem. Generally speaking, the emperor treated Jews differently than his immediate predecessors.[43] Constantine instituted policies that negatively affected them. He strengthened rules against circumcision, required Jews in the curial

---

[40] Julian, "An Edict to the Alexandrians," in *The Works of Emperor Julian*, vol. 3, trans. by W.C. Wright (Cambridge, MA: Harvard University Press, 1923).

[41] See Julian, "Letter to Ecdicius," in *The Works of Emperor Julian*, vol. 3, trans. by W.C. Wright (Cambridge, MA: Harvard University Press, 1923).

[42] Julian, "Letter to the Alexandrians," in *The Works of Emperor Julian*, vol. 3, trans. by W.C. Wright (Cambridge, MA: Harvard University Press, 1923), 435a-d.

[43] Sozomen, *Ecclesiastical History*, 4.7.5.

class to fulfill their duties, even if those duties conflicted with their religious customs. He even threatened anyone who considered converting to Judaism.[44] By contrast, Julian expressed admiration for their customs, sympathy for their previous plight and unjust subjugation under Christian rule.[45] He also took measures to ease their burden. He stopped excessive taxation, burned imperial documents regarding their impiety, and most surprisingly, asked the patriarch, Hillel II, to stop a burdensome levy used to support their religious leaders. But perhaps the great expression of admiration was his plan to rebuild the Temple. This sacred building was destroyed by the Roman army under Titus in AD 70. In the Bar Kochba revolt (132-135), Jews captured Jerusalem and made efforts to restore the Temple, but these efforts were quickly crushed by Emperor Hadrian. Early in 363,[46] Julian appointed Alypius to oversee its restoration. However, not long after construction began, reports of "repeated and alarming outburst of fire-balls near the foundations" made the project untenable, and it was abandoned.[47] Though it ended almost as quickly as it began, the project caught the attention of observers, especially Christians, who interpreted its failure through the lens of divine providence. Some even reported seeing crosses appear in the sky as the fire fell from heaven.[48]

---

[44] *Codex Theodosianus*, 16.8.1. See T.G. Elliott, *The Christianity of Constantine the Great* (Scranton, PA: University of Scranton Press, 1996), 112-13.

[45] Julian, "Letter to the Community of the Jews ," in *The Works of Emperor Julian*, vol. 3, trans. by W.C. Wright (Cambridge, MA: Harvard University Press, 1923).

[46] Though this is the traditional date, Michael Avi-Yonah suggests that the project was undertaken later in the year when Julian was already campaigning in Persia. See *Jews of Palestine: Political History from the Bar Kokhba War to the Arab Conquest* (Blackwell, 1976). For a response to Avi-Yonah, see Bowersock, *Julian the Apostate*, 120-22.

[47] Ammianus Marcellinus, *The Later Roman Empire*, 23.1.

[48] See Philostorgius, *Ecclesiastical History*, 7.9; Theodoret, *Ecclesiastical History*, 3.15.

It is rather strange that an emperor known for his animosity toward Christianity undertook such a project. Though the emperor never explicitly conveyed his reason, there are a couple of plausible explanations. Perhaps it was part of his overall project of restoring paganism. At the core of paganism (at least the version he attempted to restore) was sacrifice. One of his first acts after becoming emperor was sacrificing animals with his military troops; one of his first edicts was overturning the ban on animal sacrifice. Thus, restoring the Temple in Jerusalem might have been part of his general commitment to open temples and promote sacrifice. Julian certainly praised the Jews for their sacrificial rituals and laws (mentioned above). Various historical sources indicate the emperor even contacted Jewish authorities and demanded they resume animal sacrifice.[49] Such a request was denied. The religious authorities replied that proper religious sacrifice must be offered in the Temple. This reply possibly gave Julian reason to begin reconstruction.[50] Yet this explanation is less likely because he was almost as critical of Judaism as he was of Christianity.

An alternative reading, which appears more consistent with Julian's overall political philosophy, is that the reconstruction of the Temple in Jerusalem was an attempt to restore the legitimacy of the traditional faction of Judaism from which Christianity broke. In other words, Julian wanted to pit these sects against each other, as he did

---

[49] See "Fragment 11," in *The Works of Emperor Julian*, vol. 3, trans. by W.C. Wright (Cambridge, MA: Harvard University Press, 1923) and "Letter to a Priest," vol. 2, trans. by W.C. Wright (Cambridge, MA: Harvard University Press, 1913), 295c. The fragment's authenticity and its recipient are unclear. This ambiguity is understandable given that the author used the phrase "Most High God," which seems inconsistent with Julian's theology. Yet this same phrase appears in the emperor's letter to the Jewish community, and several ancient historians credit the fragment to Julian (see Sozomen, *Ecclesiastical History*, 5.22; Socrates, *Ecclesiastical History*, 3.20; and Theodoret, *Ecclesiastical History*, 3.15).

[50] Bowersock suggests that the Jewish authorities might even have opposed the project. See *Julian*, 89-90.

through his amnesty for orthodox clergy. In his second oration against Julian, Gregory of Nazianzus, another influential fourth century theologian, says that the attempt to rebuild the Temple was part of the emperor's plot to destroy Christianity, though the theologian did not explain exactly how that attempt would undermine it. The Apostate, he says, was "hiding his true purpose under the mark of benevolence."[51]

The destruction of the Temple in some ways validated the Christian break from Judaism. Historically, the Temple was where sacrifices were performed. Naturally, Christians argued that Jews could no longer sacrifice; the traditional expression of that religion was impossible. Constantine even attempted to transform Jerusalem into a Christian city. Among other things, he dedicated the Church of the Resurrection. These efforts were so pronounced Eusebius proclaimed the town the "New Jerusalem."[52] Christians also interpreted various biblical passages as references to the Temple's destruction. In *Hymns against Julian*, Ephrem, a fourth century theologian later declared Doctor of the Church, referenced the prophet Daniel, who said in the ninth book of his prophecy: "And after the sixty-two weeks it shall be built again with squares and moat, but in a troubled time. And after the sixty-two weeks, an anointed one shall be cut off, and shall have nothing; and the people of the prince who is to come shall destroy the city and the sanctuary. Its end shall come with a flood, and to the end there shall be war; desolations are decreed." Ephrem used this prophecy to mock the emperor's efforts to rebuild: "He [God] ordered the winds and they blew, he beckoned earthquakes and they came, lightning and it caused turmoil, the air and it became dark, walls and they were overthrown, gates and they opened themselves; fire came forth and consumed the scribes who had read in Daniel that it would be desolate for ever; and because they had read but did not learn, they

---

[51] Gregory of Nazianzus, *Second Oration against Julian*, 3.
[52] *Life of Constantine*, 3.33.

were violently smitten and then they learned!"[53] Another prophecy, this one spoken by Jesus, was also frequently referenced in regards to the Temple. Jesus says, "there will not be left here one stone upon another, that will not be thrown down."[54] The historian, Philostorgius, cited this passage, while commenting on the emperor's attempt at restoration.[55] The Apostate, he writes, attempted to discredit the prophecies of Jesus but was overruled by the truth of their claims when fire came down from heaven and an earthquake consumed those working on the Temple. That very validation of Christianity was in part tied to the destruction of the Temple. This helps explain why Christian commentators interpreted the failed reconstruction in such miraculous terms, as well as why Julian wanted to restore the Temple and Jewish sacrifice.

## The Politics of Factions

In light of Julian's overall disposition to Christianity, his religious tolerance appears almost an anomaly, especially if viewed benevolently. However, with this overall disposition in mind, his use of tolerance is better read as an attempt to multiply factions and thereby neutralize, if not subvert, the faith. The use of factions is a familiar mechanism in political philosophy. In *Discourses on Livy*, Niccolò Machiavelli credited the vitality of the Roman republic to factional politics, though he was aware of their military prowess and the aid of fortune. It was the "tumults between the nobles and the plebs," he says, that was the "first cause" or even the "best cause" of Roman success.[56] One of the major mechanisms that promoted this tumultuous and, by consequence, free republic was the ability for

---

[53] Ephrem Syrus, *Hymn against Julian*, 4.20.

[54] Matthew 24:1-2. See also Matthew 24:1-2, 15-16; Mark 13:2; and Luke 19:44, 21:6.

[55] Philstorgius, *Ecclesiastical History*, 7.9. The passage referenced is Matthew 24.2.

[56] Machiavelli, *Discourses on Livy*, 1.4. Trans. by Harvey Mansfield and Nathan Tarcov (Chicago, IL: University of Chicago Press, 1996).

citizens to vent their concerns and ambitions.[57] Machiavelli recognized that, in every republic, there are factions, or what he called "humors," and that, by using various mechanisms like this one, a republic can be stable. Other modern political philosophers also recognized the need to manage factions within a regime to promote overall stability. For example, in discussing the English constitution, both Baron Charles-Louis de Montesquieu and David Hume credited its genius to "the opposition of interests." Though it "breeds endless factions," Hume writes, "it does all the good without any of the harm."[58] Perhaps the most noted discussion of factions is found in *Federalist Paper 10*. In this essay, James Madison proposed a solution to the "mortal disease" of factional politics by suggesting that factions be multiplied, not removed. Such a step is necessary because factions, or the diverse passions of a citizenry, are sown in the nature of man and to remove them is to remove liberty. Thus, the chief architect of the U.S. Constitution recommended that the most effective way to neutralize the threat of a majority is to multiply factions.

This tactic is effective essentially because the possibility of tyranny is less likely. Tyranny often occurs when political power is controlled by one party, or in a democracy, when a majority can control minority factions. This tyranny makes plurality improbable at best and offers little to no recourse for minority factions. In a democracy, for example, the interests of the poor, who compose the majority of any population, can tyrannize the rich, unless certain institutional measures are taken to check this danger. By multiplying factions, the possibility of a tyranny of the majority is less likely. A faction possesses its own particular interests or goods that are often in competition with other factions, thus factions promote divisiveness, instead of concord. In terms of religious factions, each sect maintains its own belief about what is orthodox, a belief that is often rejected by

---

[57] Ibid., 1.7.

[58] Hume, *Idea of a Perfect Commonwealth*. For Montesquieu, see *Spirit of the Laws*, 2.11.6. Immanuel Kant and Karl Marx also saw the benefit of conflict and antagonism in the development of politics.

the other sects. This in turn promotes hostility, competition, and proselytizing amongst the different factions. In a regime that promotes factions, one party or a majority is difficult to form because the factions, pursuing their interests, serve as antagonistic stabilizers to other factions that are pursuing their interests. This makes it difficult for one faction or sect to gain the adherents necessary to acquire a majority or control political power. In the case of the Christians in Antioch, each particular sect, guided by its bishop, adhered to its own Christology: the followers of bishop Euzoius, the Arian doctrine; those faithful to Eustathius, the orthodox position; and those who accepted Meletius, their doctrine. Each sect proselytized pagans and Christians belonging to the other sects, and each sect considered other understandings of Christology mistaken. If the attempt to rebuild the Temple in Jerusalem had been successful, debates regarding the application and interpretation of Mosaic Law, especially in regards to sacrifice, would have immediately resumed.

An essential part of this tactic is supporting and strengthening minority factions in the regime in order to weaken and counterbalance the majority. If weaker factions are not adequately strengthened, and if the majority is not sufficiently constrained, the tactic is impotent. In the Roman republic, the consuls, the Senate, and the tribune of the plebs created a stable regime, as Machiavelli noted, for each guarded the other.[59] In the English Constitution, the three powers of government were separated into three branches thereby ensuring these powers were not in a single person or in a single body of the magistracy,[60] and underlying the U.S. Constitution was the natural right to private property, which was one means of protection against tyranny. In the fourth century, Arians had almost completely won. Thus, reintroduction of the near defeated orthodox was sure to cause dissension. Julian attempted to strengthen the minority Christian faction by issuing amnesty for their clergy and

---

[59] *Discourses on Livy*, 1.2.

[60] See Montesquieu's discussion of the English Constitution, *Spirit of the Laws*, 2.11.6.

sought to resurrect the obsolete sacrificial traditions of Judaism, the religion from which the majority sect sprang, by rebuilding the Temple of Jerusalem.

The commendation of factions stands juxtaposed to their disapproval, a sentiment often expressed by ancient political philosophers. Pythagoras compares factions in a city to a disease in the body. Thucydides says that faction is a fertile source for ruin.[61] In the *Republic*, Socrates says that factions are the product of injustice.[62] In order to eradicate these factions, the ancients promoted like-mindedness through policies Montesquieu said were "very painful" because they promote the common good over private interest.[63] (However, it is debatable whether Montesquieu thinks this kind of self-sacrifice is bad politically, although it is painful individually.) There is perhaps no greater example of the ancient disdain for faction than the public reforms in Sparta by Lycurgus.[64] After experiencing the ills of political disorder wrought by factions, Spartans requested that the statesman restore order. He implemented three measures that attempted to eradicate factions. First, he established the senate, which served as the stabilizing element in the regime by dividing governmental powers between the various classes. Second, he promoted economic equality by dividing the land equally amongst the citizenry by establishing iron (not gold or silver) as the regime's currency. Finally, the statesman mandated "common meals," whereby each citizen was required to eat at public tables instead of their private residence.

It might appear strange to claim that Julian, an emperor well-versed in ancient political philosophy, promoted factions. As a matter of fact, he made comments on the topic that were consistent with the ancients. For example, in a letter to an Edessan official, the emperor condemned a sect of Christians for disturbing order and exhorted

---

[61] *The Peloponnesian War*, 1.1.
[62] 351-c-d.
[63] *Spirit of the Laws*, 1.4.5.
[64] See Plutarch, *Life of Lycurgus*.

them to "abstain from all feuds and rivalries."⁶⁵ Reportedly, some Arian Christians attacked believers from another sect, the Valentinians. The emperor then ordered that all their valuables be confiscated and either given to soldiers or returned to the city for civic use. With a bit of sarcasm, he said his actions helped save their souls by forcing them to fulfill Jesus' command to "sell all you have." In another example, in the city of Bostra, Christian leaders, including the bishop, purportedly incited the faithful to revolt partly in response to their change in status under the emperor.⁶⁶ Julian exhorted the citizens, especially the Christians, to abstain from joining in the "feuds of the clerics" that lead to "disunion." He expressed similar sentiments to the Alexandrian pagans, who engaged in their own lawlessness by murdering George, the bishop of Cappadocia. According to Ammianus Marcellinus, the bishop apparently ordered a pagan temple raided and a shrine destroyed, and in turn, a pagan mob murdered three Christians, including the bishop. Julian rebuked the Alexandrians, not because of the severity of their response—he even said "I might even admit that he deserved even worse and [a] more cruel treatment," but because they broke the law. In his eyes, they should have brought George to the one who could lawfully administer punishment. Yet in their anger, he said, they promoted disorder and lawlessness.⁶⁷

---

⁶⁵ Julian, "Letter to Hecebolius," 425a.

⁶⁶ Whether Titus, the bishop of Bostra, incited the faithful is questionable. Julian admitted that Titus wrote a letter admonishing them not to cause sedition. He even quoted from the letter: "Although the Christians are a match for the Hellenes in numbers, they are restrained by our admonition that no one disturb the peace in any place" ("Letter to the Citizens of Bostra," 437d).

⁶⁷ The emperor appeared rather hypocritical in his response to their violence. Julian did not punish them but only offered a stern rebuke. According to Ammianus, he wanted to punish them, yet certain advisors persuaded him otherwise (22.11). It is difficult to say whether this is accurate or whether Ammianus was simply offering an apology. See Julian, "Letter to Hecebolius," 424c-d.

Though at times Julian rhetorically promoted order and harmony, his actions, as illustrated above, actually promoted *stasis*. There are a couple of explanations that might account for this tension. It is possible that, even though he was heavily influenced by ancient philosophy, he was guided more by political expediency than principle. Consider his personal piety as an example. At times the emperor did appear pious. Prior to accepting the office of Augustus, he consulted the gods.[68] Before marching against his cousin Constantius II, he conferred with them again.[69] He took no major action without first consulting the gods. Immediately after receiving his imperial status, Julian offered a sacrifice to Bellona, the goddess of war. Later, he boasted to his friend, Maximus, about sacrificing openly to the gods with his army.[70] The pagan historian, Ammianus Marcellinus, recorded that he sacrificed a hundred bulls and countless flocks of animals in one day.[71] His fervor for sacrifice was so great that Christians said there would be no animals left to sacrifice if he defeated the Persians.

---

[68] While stationed in Paris, his troops proclaimed him Augustus, perhaps in response to Constantius' request that over one half of the army was to leave Gaul to help the emperor in the East. Julian said he was completely surprised by this proclamation and then retreated into an upper room to seek divine guidance. He prayed to Zeus and asked for a sign. The god of thunder apparently obliged ("Letter to the Athenians," in *The Works of Emperor Julian*, vol. 2, trans. by W.C. Wright [Cambridge, MA: Harvard University Press, 1913], 284c-285a).

[69] The approval is recorded by Ammianus Marcellinus: "When Zeus had crossed Aquarius' broad domain, and Cronos reached the five and twentieth day of Virgo, then Constantius, Asia's king, shall end his life in pain and misery" (*The Later Roman Empire*, 21.2.2). See also Zosimus, *New History*, 3.9.

[70] "I worship the gods openly," he proclaimed, "and the whole mass of the troops who are returning with me worship the gods. I sacrifice oxen in public. I have offered to the gods many hecatombs as thanks-offerings" ("To Maximus, the Philosopher," in *The Works of Emperor Julian*, vol. 3, trans. W.C. Wright [Cambridge, MA: Harvard University Press, 1923], 415 c-d).

[71] Ammianus, *The Later Roman Empire*, 22.12.

At other times, however, Julian's piety seemed more utilitarian than sincere. The divine approval (or rather disapproval) of his campaign against the Persians serves as a prime example. The emperor began preparations for the campaign almost immediately after Constantius' death. Julian inherited tension with the Persians, and for whatever reason, wanted to settle it. But before leaving for battle, the emperor sought divine approval for his campaign. However, the gods did not appear amenable this time. Ammianus Marcellinus mentions several negative omens.[72] A Roman officer, Felix, suddenly died in Julian's presence; a pagan priest died on the steps of a shrine dedicated to the Genius of the Roman people. There was an earthquake in Constantinople, and a consultation of the Sibylline books, a collection of ancient sibyls and oracles, provided a definitive answer—"the emperor must not advance beyond his borders this year."[73] In direct defiance of these omens, Julian marched ahead.[74] This defiance seems uncharacteristic of a pious believer. One might excuse his lapse as a moment of weakness, but his defiance continued. Even after departing Antioch, he encountered other ill omens. A colonnade in Hierapolis suddenly collapsed, killing fifty men. While at Cercusium, Julian received a letter from the prefect of Gaul, exhorting him to cease the campaign, since the gods disapproved. The emperor ignored this warning, and at one point, crossed a bridge with his army and ordered it to be destroyed in order to ensure no one could retreat. If truly pious, it seems faithfulness to the gods would be primary, and his political will would bend to theirs. Yet it did not. Instead of bending his will to theirs, he bent their will to his by manufacturing his own divine blessing only days into the

---

[72] Ibid., 23.1.5-7.

[73] *imperatorem eo anno discedere a limitibus suis.*

[74] Theodoret suggested the gods promised Julian victory. He recorded one such oracle: "Now we gods all started to get trophies of victory by the river beast and of them I, Ares, bold raiser of the din of war, will be leader" (*Ecclesiastical History*, 3.16). The historian said "the beast" was a reference to the Tigris and victory over the Persians. It could be the signs conflicted, but at least as far as I know, no other source credited a blessing to the campaign.

campaign.⁷⁵ After reaching Beroea, he consulted the gods himself. Unsurprisingly, Zeus declared the campaign auspicious.⁷⁶ Perhaps earlier interpreters read the Sibylline books improperly; perhaps all the previous omens were mere coincidence; or perhaps Julian created his own blessing in hopes of appeasing the pagan populace. An emperor cannot afford to defy the gods so openly after all. It appears that Julian was pious, when religion was beneficial; impious, when it was not.⁷⁷ If Julian placed political expediency above his faithfulness to the gods, it certainly seems that ignoring the wisdom of ancient philosophy for such expediency would not be out of the realm of possibility.

It is also possible his use of factions was essential to achieving the greater harmony of the regime. Christianity was a disease for Julian, a disease that needed to be removed before Roman vitality

---

⁷⁵ Those who interpret Julian's piety in a more sincere and straightforward manner might object to such a cynical reading of the statesman, but these same scholars almost unanimously acknowledge such dubiousness in regards to Julian's Christian pretensions. Befitting a nephew of the Emperor Constantine, Julian was baptized and raised Christian, but for roughly a decade, the future Augustus hid his own paganism. He served as a lector at the church in Nicomedia and attended Mass on the Feast of the Epiphany as late as 361. One might respond that such cover was necessary for survival, and this was probably the case. Yet this demonstrates his willingness to participate in religious rituals, not out of sincerity or for their truthfulness, but for their usefulness, in this case, self-preservation.

⁷⁶ The emperor again invoked Zeus, who this time provided a sign from heaven. Julian later sacrificed a white bull to the god, no doubt in thanksgiving for his divine acquiescence. See Julian, "Letter to Libanius," in *The Works of Emperor Julian*, vol. 3, trans. by W.C. Wright (Cambridge, MA: Harvard University Press, 1923), 399d.

⁷⁷ This attitude seems strikingly similar to the behavior suggested centuries later by Machiavelli. "[B]y appearing to have them," he writes, "they are useful, as it is to appear . . . religious, and to be so, but to remain with a spirit built so that, if you need not to be those things, you are able and know how to change to the contrary" (*The Prince*, trans. by Harvey Mansfield [Chicago, IL: University of Chicago Press, 1998], 18).

could return, and hence much like a doctor who cures a patient by turning the disease against itself, he pitted Christian sects against one another in order to cure the regime.

## Conclusion

Regardless of how the tension between Julian's promotion of order and his use of factions is resolved, his religious tolerance appears anything but benevolent. As a matter of fact, given his overall disposition to Christianity, it appears that it was a mechanism to multiply factions and thus neutralize, if not subvert, what he perceived as a political threat. If this reading is correct, Julian instituted a more subtle means than the violent persecutions ordered by his predecessors in order to rid Rome of a religious threat. Instead of the state inflicting violence upon Christians, his use of factions allowed Christians to inflict harm on themselves.

In this way, Julian appears ahead of his time. Similar to those political philosophers calling for religious tolerance in the early modern period, the emperor sought a way to end religious violence and restore political order. And if I can be somewhat bold, it seems the Apostate's same subversive intent can be found in some of his philosophic successors. To be sure, Christians calling for tolerance had no such aim. They simply sought refuge from persecution, state or otherwise. Yet others had reason to subvert religion because of its perceived unsettling effect on political order. In his essay, "What is Enlightenment?," Immanuel Kant described how humanity would one day emerge from its "self-incurred immaturity."[78] At the core of this progress was freedom, freedom to make use of one's reason in all matters, especially religious ones. This would enable humanity to work its way out of religious barbarism to enlightenment. Thomas Jefferson offered similar logic: "Reason and free enquiry are the only effectual agents against error. Give a loose to them, they will support

---

[78] In *Political Writings*, ed. by H.S. Reiss (New York, NY: Cambridge University Press, 1991), 54-60.

the true religion, by bringing every false one to their tribunal."[79] Likewise, John Stuart Mill recommended the civic use of a "Religion of Humanity," which in his eyes was superior to revealed religions, such as Christianity and Islam.[80] Such a "religion" could only emerge through means suggested by Kant and Jefferson, namely "the liberty of thought and discussion."[81] Thus, in the history of political thought, it appears philosophers found a more effective means than outright persecution for neutralizing a religion that threatens the order and stability of a regime. And it seems Julian was one of the first to discover (and implement) this tactic.

---

[79] *Notes on the State of Virginia*, 17.

[80] "Utility of Religion," in *The Collected Works of John Stuart Mill, vol. 10: Essays on Ethics, Religion, and Society*, ed. by John Robson (New York, NY: Routledge, 1996).

[81] The title of the second chapter in Mill's *On Liberty*.

# 3

## CALVERT, WILLIAMS, AND LOCKE: THREE FOUNDATIONS FOR RELIGIOUS TOLERATION IN AMERICA

*Maura Jane Farrelly*

Religious toleration is very un-American. As a people, we do not—technically—*tolerate* various religious faiths. To do so, after all, would be to assume that there is a right and universally knowable answer when it comes to the question of whether there is an all-powerful Creator, and if so, what the proper relationship between that Creator and humanity should be. In America, we do not say (at least constitutionally) that people have the freedom to be wrong. That would be religious toleration. Leaving aside the rhetorical (though, for some atheists, not insignificant) references to "God," "Nature's God," and a "Creator" in the Pledge of Allegiance, the Declaration of Independence, and on our currency, the fact is that in America we skirt the issue of whether there is a right answer to the God question.[1]

---

[1] Michael Newdow is an atheist who has devoted himself to eradicating these rhetorical references to "God." He has filed lawsuits challenging the use of the word "God" in the Pledge of Allegiance, on America's currency, and during the inaugural ceremonies for American presidents. In all of these cases, the courts have refused to claim that the existence of God is right, factual, or correct, even as they have ruled against Newdow. In 2002, a federal appeals court in California ruled that the Pledge was, in fact, unconstitutional because it includes the phrase "under God." That decision was later thrown out by the U.S. Supreme Court, however, not because the judges believed the nation does, in fact, exist "under God," but because Newdow did not have standing in the case, since he was not the custodial parent of the schoolgirl whose civil rights were said to be violated. In a subsequent challenge to the Pledge that Newdow, who is an attorney,

We do not commit. Instead, we say that all answers have their place in America. What we embrace is religious *liberty*.

"It is no more that toleration is spoken of as if it were the indulgence of one class of people, that another enjoyed the exercise of their inherent natural rights."[2] These were the words of George Washington, which he proudly shared with the members of the Touro Synagogue in Newport, Rhode Island, in March of 1790. In saying this, Washington was really expressing a wish, rather than making a statement about reality, as Jews were still not allowed to vote or hold office in Rhode Island, suggesting that the legal culture there did still view the Jewish answer as "wrong" on some level, and that when they attended worship services openly at their synagogue in

---

brought on behalf of other parents in California, the Ninth Circuit Court ruled that the Pledge does not violate the First Amendment to the Constitution, so long as districts allow children and employees to opt out of saying all or part of it. In 2006, a federal judge in California rejected Newdow's claim that the phrase "In God We Trust" on America's currency was a violation of the First Amendment, saying that the phrase is "ceremonial" and therefore "secular." The Supreme Court refused to hear Newdow's appeal of that decision. In 2009, then, a federal judge in the District of Columbia rejected Newdow's challenge to the use of the word "God" in presidential inaugural ceremonies, on the grounds that Newdow had failed to show how atheists are "harmed" by the word's usage in the ceremony. See Evelyn Nieves, "Judges Ban Pledge of Allegiance from Schools, Citing 'Under God,'" (*New York Times*, June 26th, 2002); Linda Greenhouse, "8 Justices Block Effort to Excise Phrase in Pledge," (*New York Times*, June 14th, 2004); Associated Press, "Court won't hear challenge to 'In God We Trust,'" (Washington Post, March 7th, 2011); Reggie B. Walton, United States District Court, District of Columbia, Case 1.08-cv-02248-RBW, Document 74, 2.

[2] George Washington to the Hebrew Congregation of Newport, August 18, 1790 in Jonathan D. Sarna and David G. Dalin, eds. *Religion and State in the American Jewish Experience* (Notre Dame, IN: University of Notre Dame Press, 1997), 79–80.

Newport, Jews were being "indulged" by their Christian neighbors, in spite of the president's words to the contrary.³

But Washington was certainly not alone in disdaining toleration as a mere indulgence and questioning its validity, then, as a foundation for the new republic. His home state of Virginia had disestablished the Episcopal Church four years before he addressed the Jews in Newport, and in December of 1791, Virginia became the eleventh state to approve the Third Article in the Bill of Rights, amending the U.S. Constitution for the very first time and formally preventing the federal government from ever establishing that there was a "right" answer when it came to the question of God.⁴

In spite of the overwhelming support that the First Amendment enjoyed among state lawmakers, it took a while for some leaders to adopt Washington's posture toward toleration when it came to religious matters that were local. Lawmakers in Rhode Island, for instance, did not extend the rights of full citizenship to non-Christians until 1798, when they enacted a statute "relative to religious freedom and the maintenance of ministers." Neighboring Massachusetts did not abolish its laws requiring residents to pay a tax to support the Congregational Church (or, to be fair, some other church of their choosing; Congregationalists merely enjoyed the benefits of being the official default) until 1833. And in New

---

³ Patrick T. Conley, "Rhode Island: Laboratory for 'The Lively Experiment,'" in *The Bill of Rights and the States: The Colonial and Revolutionary Origins of American Liberties*, ed. Patrick T. Conley and John P. Kaminski (Madison, WI: Madison House Publishers, 1992), 131-132.

⁴ The Third Article in the Bill of Rights became the First Amendment to the U.S. Constitution, as the First Article—which addresses the issue of apportionment in the House of Representatives—has still not achieved the approval of three-fourths of the states, and the Second Article—which addresses the issue of congressional salaries—was not approved by the states until 1992, when it became the Twenty-Seventh Amendment. See Gordon Lloyd, "The Four States of Approval of the Bill of Rights in Congress and the States," TeachingAmericanHistory.org, retrieved September 15th, 2014, http://teachingamericanhistory.org/bor/four-stages/.

Hampshire and New Jersey, in spite of Article Six of the U.S. Constitution, whereby religious tests for officeholders were outlawed on the federal level, state and municipal authorities were required to be Protestants until well into the 1870s.[5]

But the existence of religious tests and denominational taxes actually obscures the reality that the nineteenth century was the period when Americans slowly began to gravitate toward the idea that religious *toleration* was not what their country was all about, even if their sense of what religious *liberty* should look like, legally and culturally, was not always clear or consistent. Scholars have noted that as Methodists grew from three percent to thirty percent of the population, and Catholics flooded the ports of New York and Boston, and converted Mormon immigrants made their way from Denmark and Sweden to the Midwest, the leaders of vanguard denominations like Congregationalism and Episcopalianism gradually stopped using the word "dissenters" to describe the religious diversity they were powerless to prevent.[6] They stopped, in other words, speaking of those who were not a part of the so-called mainstream as having beliefs that were deviations from official "truth" in America.

To be sure, the ecumenism that Congregationalists and Episcopalians exhibited in the nineteenth century was bestowed far more readily on Protestants like the Methodists than it was on Catholics and Mormons, as evidenced by Archbishop John Hughes' struggles in the 1840s with the Public School Society of New York over the use of

---

[5] Patrick T. Conley and Robert G. Flanders, Jr., *The Oxford Commentaries on State Constitutions: Rhode Island* (Oxford University Press: New York, 2011), 65; Paul Finkelman, ed. *The Encyclopedia of American Civil Liberties*, Volume I (Routledge: New York, 2006), 136.

[6] Chris Beneke, *Beyond Toleration: The Religious Origins of American Pluralism* (Oxford University Press: New York, 2006), 114. Methodists made up about 2.5% of the population at the dawn of the American Revolution; by 1850, they were 34% of the American population. See Mark A. Noll, *A History of Christianity in the United States and Canada* (William B. Eerdman's Publishing Company: Grand Rapids, MI, 1992), 153.

Protestant bibles in New York City's classrooms.[7] Governor Lilburn Boggs' "Executive Order 44," which he issued in Missouri in 1838 and used to define Mormons as "enemies" who "must be exterminated or driven from the State," also serves as an important reminder that in antebellum America, some people were not willing to embrace even religious toleration as George Washington understood it—let alone religious liberty.[8]

Nevertheless, one of the well-documented, defining features of religion in the new American republic was the frequency with which Americans moved from one denomination to another. The country's religious landscape was a veritable "marketplace" in which ministers competed with one another for the attentions of a population that was not indifferent to the idea of religion, but did exhibit a growing indifference to some of the practices and even doctrines that separated one denomination from another.[9] These practices and doctrines answered questions that were increasingly irrelevant to Americans, such as whether the Sabbath fell on a Saturday or Sunday, whether carpets were an appropriate luxury to have in a house of God, and whether a proper baptism needed to involve "sprinkling" or "dunking."[10] The French immigrant J. Hector St. John de Crèvecoeur

---

[7] Diane Ravitch, *The Great School Wars: A History of the New York City Public Schools* (Johns Hopkins University Press: Baltimore, 2000; orig., 1974), 33-78.

[8] William G. Hartley, "Missouri's 1838 Extermination Order and the Mormons' Forced Removal to Illinois," *Mormon Historical Studies* 2, no. 1 (2001): 5-27; Gustav Niebuhr, "All Need Toleration: Some Observations about Recent Differences in the Experiences of Religious Minorities in the United States and Western Europe," *Annals of the American Academy of Political and Social Science* 612 (July, 2007): 174.

[9] Roger Finke and Rodney Stark, *The Churching of America, 1776-2005: Winners and Losers in Our Religious Economy* (Rutgers University Press: New Brunswick, NJ, 2006), 55-116; Nathan O. Hatch, *The Democratization of American Christianity* (Yale University Press: New Haven, 1989), 64.

[10] Hatch, ibid., 65; Maura Jane Farrelly, "Asceticism," in Jason E. Vickers, ed., *The Cambridge Companion to American Methodism* (Cambridge: New York, 2013), 218; Daniel C. Goodwin, "'The Very Vitals of

believed Americans were simply too busy to care about such questions. "The seasons call for their attention," he observed of his fellow farmers in upstate New York. They "have no time" for what he called "the foolish vanity, or rather the fury of making Proselytes." Their beliefs, he insisted, had become a "strange religious medley" that was "neither pure Catholicism nor pure Calvinism."[11]

This "religious medley" developed first in the mid to late eighteenth century, in the rural south and along the western frontier, where church infrastructures were weak and visits from clergymen, regardless of denomination, were infrequent opportunities for welcomed sociability.[12] By the dawn of the nineteenth century, however, the unwillingness of many Protestants to ascribe importance to the doctrinal differences that separated denominations had become so commonplace on college campuses in the northeast, that Timothy Dwight, president of Yale College, lamented the misguided politeness of his students, noting sarcastically that they believed "we ought never, wound an innocent man's feelings in company, especially with regard to his religious sentiments."[13]

Some scholars believe this polite ecumenism, nurtured over many decades, may be partially responsible for the astonishing degree

---

Christianity': The Baptismal Controversy and the Intellectual Awakening in Nova Scotia, 1811-1848," *Nova Scotia Historical Review* 15, no. 2 (1995): 72-87.

[11] J. Hector St. John Crèvcoeur, *Letters from an American Farmer*, 1782, rpt. (Fox, Duffield, and Co.: New York, 1904), 64-65.

[12] Finke and Stark, *The Churching of America*, 34; Curtis D. Johnson, "'Sectarian Nation': Religious Diversity in Antebellum America," *OAH Magazine* 22, no. 1 (2008): 14-18; Bridget Ford, "Beyond Cane Ridge," *Ohio Valley History* 8 no. 4 (2008): 17-37. Andrew H. M. Stern has shown that in the rural south, even the mighty denominational wall between Protestantism and Catholicism was sometimes porous. Protestants were not necessarily willing to become Catholics—but they did send their children to Catholic schools when those were the only schools available. See Stern, *Southern Crucifix, Southern Cross: Catholic-Protestant Relations in the Old South* (University of Alabama Press: Tuscaloosa, 2012).

[13] Quoted in Beneke, *Beyond Toleration*, 173.

of religious illiteracy that characterizes modern-day America.[14] A recent survey conducted by the Pew Forum on Religion and Public Life revealed that only half of all Americans today who identify as "Christian" are able to name the four Gospels of the Bible. More than half of the survey's participants who described themselves as Protestants were not able to identify Martin Luther as the theologian who had launched the Protestant Reformation, and forty-five percent of the survey's self-described Catholics did not realize that a fundamental teaching of their faith is that the bread and wine used in the Sacrament of the Eucharist are literally the body and blood of Christ.[15]

People were executed in early-modern England for refusing to give up their belief in this Doctrine of Transubstantiation that now nearly half of America's Catholics do not understand—suggesting that the polite ecumenism that took root in the United States in the nineteenth century and de-emphasized the ecclesiological and doctrinal differences between religious groups may be responsible for more than just the development of a level of ignorance that hinders our ability to have cultural conversations. It may also be responsible for the astonishing degree of peace and unanimity that we now enjoy in the most religiously diverse country in the industrial world.

Certainly our polite ecumenism—that is to say, our painstakingly developed cultural unwillingness to declare that there is a right answer to the question of how Christians should baptize a convert or when they should honor the Sabbath—played a role in the Supreme Court's decision in *Everson v. Board of Education* to apply the Bill of Rights to laws that are passed on the state level, effectively barring all governments in the United States from ever establishing

---

[14] Stephen Prothero, *Religious Literacy: What Every American Needs to Know—and Doesn't* (Harper Collins: New York, 2007), 109-154.

[15] Laurie Goodstein, "Basic Religion Test Stumps Many Americans," New York *Times*, September 28th, 2010; "Who Knows What About Religion," *Pew Research Religion and Public Life Project*, retrieved September 26th, 2014, http://www.pewforum.org/2010/09/28/u-s-religious-knowledge-survey-who-knows-what-about-religion/.

that there is a right answer to questions that touch upon humanity's relationship with God. Justice Tom Clark drew upon this 1947 decision when—in his 1960 *Abington v. Shempp* ruling on school prayer—he affirmed that the Constitution "requires the state to be neutral in its relations with groups of religious believers and non-believers." Tellingly, Clark issued this decision in spite of his personal belief that Christianity was democracy's greatest philosophical companion, and that if you "teach a nation Christianity… they will exercise tireless patience to maintain an enduring peace for people everywhere."[16]

In the years that have followed these landmark decisions, the courts (if not always the people) have been grappling with the issue of whether a particular government has actually said that there is a "right" answer to the God question when it has placed a nativity scene on a municipal lawn, for instance, or allowed a coach to lead a prayer before a public school football game. What the courts have not been grappling with is the question of whether any government should be permitted to say that there is a "right" answer, even if it also allows its citizens to be wrong. The answer to that question has been a definitive "no," as evidenced by the pains that Chief Justice Warren Berger went to in 1984 to clarify the court's opinion, when it ruled that the city of Pawtucket, Rhode Island, could continue to have a crèche—alongside Santa and his reindeer—in its annual Christmas holiday display.

"Our history is pervaded by the acknowledgement of the role of religion in American life," Berger wrote. That history gave a "secular purpose" to Pawtucket's display, even though it featured characters

---

[16] "School District of Abington Township v. Schempp, 364 U.S. 298, " *Find Law*, retrieved on September 30th, 2014 http://caselaw.lp.findlaw.com/scripts/ getcase.pl?court=US&vol=364&invol=298. Clark's quote about Christianity comes from his address to the International Sunday School Convention in Des Moines, IA, in 1947 and is quoted in Alexander Wohl, *Father, Son, and Constitution: How Justice Tom Clark and Attorney General Ramsey Clark Shaped American Democracy* (University of Kansas Press: Lawrence, KS, 2013), 176.

that some religious groups consider to be holy. The city was not answering the question of whether God exists or what humanity's relationship with God should be; it was, rather, seeking to "depict the origins" of a holiday that was "recognized by Congress and national tradition." Any "benefit to one faith or religion or all religions" that the crèche may have conveyed was entirely "incidental," according to Berger, and the display was "no more an advancement or endorsement of religion than… the exhibition of religious paintings in governmentally supported museums."[17]

But the fact that the American story is one of religious *liberty* does not mean that religious *toleration*—as an idea and as a reality—is insignificant to the country's legal and cultural development. George Washington could not have scorned toleration and dismissed it as a proper foundation for the new country had he not had the benefit of studying toleration's argument and witnessing its incarnation. Indeed, without religious toleration, there probably could not have been religious liberty in America.

In the century that preceded the American Revolution, three Englishmen articulated similar, but ultimately different arguments for religious toleration that each played roles in America's cultural development. All three men believed that there were "wrong" answers to the God question—which is why what they called for must be seen as "toleration," rather than "liberty." One of the three, however, articulated an argument for religious toleration that was deeply epistemological, and which thoroughly privatized religious belief. The fact that this argument was the one embraced by Founders such as Thomas Jefferson and James Madison is the reason that religious toleration was able to evolve into religious liberty in the United States.

---

[17] "Lynch v. Donnelly, 465 U.S. 668 (1984)," *Find Law*, retieved September 30th, 2014 http://caselaw.lp.findlaw.com/scripts/getcase.pl?court=US&vol=465&invol=668 .

The three men were Roger Williams, the founder of Rhode Island and Providence Plantations; Cecilius Calvert, the founder of Maryland and the author of the first act of religious toleration in the English-speaking world; and John Locke, the author of *A Letter Concerning Toleration*, which had a great deal of influence on Thomas Jefferson's "Bill for Establishing Religious Freedom," which, in turn, served as a model for the First Amendment.[18]

All three men were motivated by a common desire, which Roger Williams alluded to in the first line of his plea for religious toleration, written in 1644: "The blood of so many hundred thousand souls of Protestants and Papists, spilt in the wars of present and former ages, for their respective consciences" was, according to Williams, "not required or accepted by Jesus Christ, the prince of peace."[19]

The seventeenth century was a bloody century. Wars between and among various Christian denominations were waged in Austria, Bohemia, Denmark, France, Germany, Ireland, Scotland, Switzerland, and, of course, England. Catholics strangled and burned Mennonites in what is now Belgium. Protestants disemboweled and then hanged Jesuit priests in Scotland. In France, Calvinists forced Catholics to eat their own testicles, and Catholics, then, slaughtered Calvinists in the streets, in a massacre that lasted for several weeks, and that Protestant and Catholic historians still cannot agree upon, as far as the death toll is concerned.

Williams was tired of it, and so, too, was John Locke, who lamented—45 years after Williams published his *Bloudy Tenent of Persecution for Cause of Conscience*—that "firey zealots" did "persecute, torment, destroy, and kill other men upon pretence of religion." Locke scoffed at the idea that it was out of "love to men's souls" that

---

[18] Sanford Kessler, "Locke's Influence on Jefferson's Bill for Establishing Religious Freedom," *Journal of Church and State*, 25 no. 2 (1983): 231-252.

[19] Roger Williams, *The Bloudy Tenent of Persecution for Cause of Consenscience* (1644), Samuel L. Caldwell, ed. (Narragansett Club: Providence, RI, 1867), 3.

such zealots would "deprive them of their estates, maim them with corporal punishments, starve and torment them in noisome prisons and in the end even take away their lives." If this was done, he wondered, "to make men Christian and procure their salvation," why, then, did zealots "suffer whoredom, fraud, malice, and other enormities" that were "certainly more contrary to the glory of God, to the purity of the church, and to the salvation of souls than any conscientious dissent from ecclesiastical decisions."[20]

Cecilius Calvert was equally frustrated with the violence and destruction that inevitably resulted when people of different faiths could not get along. Unlike Williams and Locke, however, he did not have the freedom to write tomes about the costs of religious intolerance. Calvert was an English Catholic, and in the seventeenth century, pretty much anything a Catholic in England might say about religion was interpreted as "popery" and "papist tyranny." Nevertheless, it is telling that Calvert issued his "Act Concerning Religion" in 1649, one year after the conclusion of a nasty conflict in Maryland that pitted Protestants against Catholics and during which 80 percent of the colony's white population either fled or was killed. That act not only prohibited the government from penalizing people for practicing their faith, it also punished anyone who said anything derogatory about the belief system of another individual.[21]

The earliest English advocates of religious toleration wanted peace. And the reason they wanted peace was that violence and bloodshed are decidedly unpleasant. But each man wanted peace for other reasons, as well. And it is when we dissect these other reasons that we come to understand the difference between religious "toleration" and religious "liberty," and why it is that some approaches to toleration are more prone to evolve into liberty than others.

---

[20] John Locke, *A Letter Concerning Toleration* (1689), W. Popple, trans. (J. Brook: London, 1796), 6-7.

[21] Maura Jane Farrelly, *Papist Patriots: The Making of an American Catholic Identity* (Oxford University Press: New York, 2012), 96-99.

## Williams

Roger Williams was not a religious pluralist. He was a hardcore Baptist who got kicked out of Massachusetts because, among other things, he thought Puritan leaders there were not holding people to a high enough standard when it came to qualifying for church membership.[22] Roger Williams knew that there was a "right" answer to the God question. It was a version of the answer that John Calvin had formulated in Geneva roughly one hundred years earlier. And make no mistake—Williams wanted other people to understand that there was a "right" answer, too. This is one of the reasons he was such a great advocate of religious toleration.

"A civil sword," Williams wrote in his *Bloudy Tenent*, "is so far from bringing or helping forward an opposite in religion to repentance"—i.e., "a conversion"—"that magistrates sin grievously against the work of God and blood of souls by such proceedings." The reason the sword was not a good tool whereby to effect a conversion was obvious, according to Williams. "The sufferings of false and Antichristian teachers harden their followers, who being blind, by this means are occasioned to tumble into the ditch of hell after their blind leaders with more inflamed zeal."[23]

Persecution, in other words, fed ignorance and zealotry. The problem was not just that civil laws were ineffective when it came to conversion; it was that they actively worked against conversion, by encouraging people to identify more strongly with their persecuted leaders and reminding them of the reasons they had chosen to adopt a

---

[22] Williams' standards for church membership have not survived, so we do not know what they were. But he was notorious in Massachusetts for his criticism of what he considered to be the "lax" standards of membership. According to John Winthrop, governor of the Massachusetts Bay Colony, not long after he was banished, Williams told his friends and neighbors that he believed he and his wife were the only people he knew who were qualified to belong to a church. See Edmund S. Morgan, *Visible Saints: The History of a Puritan Idea* (Cornell University Press: Ithaca, NY, 1965), 109.

[23] Williams, *Bloudy Tenent*, 138-139.

particular "erronious and blind conscience" in the first place. Just as you would not use something as ethereal as an "exhortation to repent and be baptized" to "batter downe a stronghold, high wall, fort, tower, or castle," good Christians—that is, individuals who possessed what Williams called a "conscience rightly informed"—should not use "cannons... bullets, powder, muskets, [and] swords" to "batter downe idolatry, false worship, heresie, [and] schism."[24]

The state needed to stop persecuting people for their religious beliefs, not because there was not a "right" answer, but because persecution made it harder for people who knew that answer to help those who were still wallowing in ignorance come to the truth.[25] Williams' high standards for church membership did cause him to doubt whether most Christians—even himself—were really qualified to use what he called "spiritual artillery" (i.e., Scripture, or "the Word of God") against "false" and "Antichristian" belief. "Woe be to me if I call light darkness, and darkness light," he wrote in 1645, when explaining his own hesitancy to devote himself to the conversion of the Narragansett Indians in his region of New England. Nevertheless, Williams fervently believed that "the followers of Jesus are now the only people of God," and that it was, therefore, God's wish that the Narragansett would one day come to know Christ. "I hope in the

---

[24] Ibid., 42, 148.

[25] Interestingly, Williams seemed to imply that there were shades of truth between the "right" answer—which was Calvinist Christianity—and the "wrong" answer, which was no religion at all. One of the reasons he deplored civil laws that commanded uniformity in religion was that such laws not only failed to bring about legitimate conversions, but they also prevented people who worshipped with "erroneous consciences" from exploring and developing their mistaken beliefs, leaving them with "no Religion at all, all their dayes," a condition that was "worse then the very Indians, who dare not live without Religion according to as they are perswaded." See ibid., 290.

Lords time shall be, thousands truly converted from Antichristian Idols," he wrote, "to serve the living and true God."[26]

## Calvert

The "true God" the Narragansett needed to serve was, of course, a Protestant one. As a Baptist, Roger Williams put Catholics in the same category as "Jews and Turkes;" all three needed to be converted.[27] But had he been living in Maryland in the mid-seventeenth century, Williams might have had some difficulty showing Catholics the error of their ways, even if he did so as a private individual, rather than as a representative of the government. One of the things that caused Protestants like Williams to view the "Christian" identity of Catholics with suspicion, after all, was the status of Mary in Catholic doctrine and piety. The "Act Concerning Religion," however, made it illegal for anyone in Maryland to "use or utter any reproachful words or speeches concerning the blessed virgin Mary the mother of our savior."[28] Although the law was only ever sporadically enforced, its existence might have made it difficult for a Calvinist like Williams to convince Catholics that they were wrong to

---

[26] Ibid., 148; Roger Williams, *Christenings Make not Christians; or A brief discourse concerning that name heathen commonly given the Indians* (Iane Coe: London, 1645), 3, 14,14.

[27] Williams understood that some Protestants were willing to consider Catholic countries to be a part of "Christendom," albeit an extremely wayward part. He, however, insisted that Catholics "hath no more of Christ then the name," and the term he used for them was "unconverted and unchristian Christians." Ibid., 6-8.

[28] "Act Concerning Religion," a.k.a., "Maryland Toleration Act, September 21, 1649," *The Avalon Project: Documents in Law, History, and Diplomacy*, Lillian Goldman Law Library, Yale Law School, retrieved October 21st, 2014, http://avalon.law.yale.edu/18th_century/maryland_toleration.asp .

venerate the mother of Jesus, if such a suggestion could be considered "reproachful."²⁹

The "Act Concerning Religion" is a difficult document to pin down. It is frequently referred to nowadays as the "Maryland Toleration Act," because during its short life, it essentially guaranteed that there would be no state-supported church in Maryland—a truly radical idea in the English-speaking world at the time. Yet, the "Act Concerning Religion" also called for the execution of anyone who denied the Trinity or the divinity of Christ – and even though no one in Maryland was ever executed for being non-Christian, and the only person arrested for blasphemy under the act, a Portuguese Jew named Jacob Lombrozo, was released after he showed that he had sworn his loyalty to the proprietor, the provision calling for the execution of non-Christians does make it difficult for some people (most particularly the Jewish students I teach at Brandeis University) to see much "toleration" in the act at all.³⁰

Additionally, as was mentioned earlier, Cecilius Calvert does not explain his motives in the document. He wrote no paeans to peace, the way Roger Williams and John Locke did. He was the Catholic proprietor of a predominantly Protestant colony, beholden first to an Anglican king, Charles I, and then to a Puritan Protector, Oliver Cromwell, after a group of Calvinists in Parliament executed Charles

---

²⁹ John Calvin preached that Catholicism's veneration of Mary was a "disrespectful" violation of Mary's own example, insisting that in the Gospel of Luke, Jesus' mother "makes herself nothing, and praises God alone." Catholics, he insisted, "idly adorn her with empty devices, and reckon almost as nothing the benefits which she received from God. They heap up an abundance of magnificent and very presumptuous titles, such as 'Queen of Heaven, Star of Salvation, [and] Gate of Life, Sweetness, Hope, and Salvation.'" See his "Luke 1:46-50" in *Commentaies on the Harmony of the Evangelists, Matthew, Mark, and Luke*, William Pringle, trans. (Calvin Translation Society: Edinburgh, 1845), available at *Christian Classics Ethereal Library*, retrieved on October 21ˢᵗ, 2014 <http://www.ccel.org/ccel/calvin/calcom31.ix.ix.html .

³⁰ Farrelly, *Papist Patriots*, 109-110.

I for being a "crypto-Catholic." The colony Calvert was responsible for was bordered on the south by a group of angry Protestant Virginians who had worked hard, but unsuccessfully, to ensure that he did not receive the charter for Maryland in 1632. These same Virginians were constantly on the look-out for reasons to give Parliament for why Maryland's charter should be revoked.[31]

Calvert was also a man who was looking to make money. His father had died deeply in debt, thanks to an earlier, failed colonial experiment up in what is now Newfoundland, and Cecilus Calvert was responsible for that debt. He had also sunk more than £20,000 of his own money into the founding of Maryland, at a time when the median estate value there was just £50.[32] It seems reasonable, therefore, to think that Calvert was not going to write anything about religion that might get in the way of his ability to make money off of the tobacco being grown in the area around the Chesapeake.

And so it is telling, in many respects, that the "Act Concerning Religion" was written at all. For the first fifteen years of Maryland's existence, Calvert tried to get away with *not* writing it. He had his brother, who was the colony's governor, instruct the Catholic minority to practice their faith quietly, so as not to antagonize Protestants, and then he simply made no arrangements for the

---

[31] Edward Fox, "Tales of the City: Head of a Divine Cult; Followers Keep Faith with the Spirit of Charles I," *The Independent (London)*, February 1st, 1995; Arnold Oskar Meyer, "Charles I and Rome," American Historical Review, 19 no. 1 (1913): 13-26; Farrelly, *Papist Patriots*, 59, 61, 91-92.

[32] Ibid., 58-59; Cecilius Calvert, *The Lord Baltemore's Case, Concerning the Province of Maryland, adjoining to Virginia in America, With full and clear Answers to all material Objections, touching his Rights, Jurisdiction, and Proceedings there, And Certaine Reasons of State, why the Parliament should not impeach the same* (1653) in Clayton Colman Hall, ed., Narratives of Early Maryland, 1633-1684 (Charles Scribner's Sons: New York, 1910), 169; Michael Graham, "Meetinghouse and Chapel: Religion and Community in Seventeenth Century Maryland," in Lois Green Carr, Philip D. Morgan, and Jean B. Russo, ed., *Colonial Chesapeake Society* (University of North Carolina Press: Chapel Hill, 1988), 268-269.

Anglican Church to be established in Maryland, so that Catholics there would not be forced to pay recusancy fines, as they were in England.[33]

But that passive plan did not work. Protestants in Maryland rebelled against the proprietor's authority and the authority of the Catholics whom he had placed in the governor's office and the Proprietary Assembly. Maryland's economy was devastated by the Ingle-Claiborne Rebellion of 1648. Robert Ingle, William Claiborne, and their followers managed to inflict more than £10,000 in property damage before Maryland's governor subdued them and executed Ingle—who, unlike Claiborne, had not even been a resident of the colony. He was the captain of a merchant ship, the *Reformation*, that did business along what is now called the Delmarva Peninsula.[34]

And so after things had calmed down, Calvert pushed a bill through Maryland's assembly that not only promised all Christians they would be able to practice their faith without interference from the government, it also wrote "mannerliness" into law. The act banned a long list of nasty terms that did nothing but make people angry, sow discord, and keep the Anglican, Calvinist, and Catholic tobacco farmers in Maryland from working together to make money: "Antinomian," "Roundhead," "Popish Priest," "Jesuit," "Jesuited Papist," "Presbyterian," "Anabaptist," "Puritan," the list went on.

Unlike Roger Williams, Cecilius Calvert *was* a religious pluralist of sorts—not because he did not think there was a "right" answer to the God question (he was, after all, a Catholic), but because he recognized that pluralism could be profitable. There was no way Maryland was ever going to be a primarily Catholic colony; the

---

[33] "Lord Baltimore's Instructions to Colonists," November 13th, 1633, in John Wesley Murray Lee, ed. *The Calvert Papers* (Peabody Publication Fund: Baltimore, 1889), 1:132.

[34] Lois Green Carr, "Sources of Political Stability and Upheaval in Seventeenth-Century Maryland," *Maryland Historical Magazine* 79 (1984): 55; Timothy B. Riordan, *The Plundering Time: Maryland and the English Civil War, 1645-46* (The Maryland Historical Society: Baltimore, 2004), 320-323.

Catholic population in England simply was not large enough to support that.[35] So Calvert needed Protestants to live in Maryland if the colony was going to make him money. But he also wanted his co-religionists—who had the "right" answer—to be able to live there, too, and to practice their faith freely while they, like the Protestants (who hardly agreed amongst themselves when it came to matters of faith), grew and sold tobacco, paid their taxes, and made themselves and their proprietor rich.

## John Locke

Cecilius Calvert is not the only figure in American history to recognize that pluralism can be profitable. In his *Notes on the State of Virginia*, Thomas Jefferson commented on the religious diversity in other parts of the country. "Our sister states of Pennsylvania and New York... have long subsisted without any establishment at all," he noted—failing to include Maryland in his observation, since Calvert's dreams of a prosperous toleration there had been short-lived, brought to an end in 1702 by King William III's establishment of the Anglican Church in the colony. "The experiment was new and doubtful when they made it," Jefferson acknowledged about the absence of an official religion in Pennsylvania and New York. "It has answered beyond conception. They flourish infinitely... Their harmony is unparalleled and can be ascribed to nothing but their unbounded tolerance."[36]

---

[35] Historians estimate that during the first half of the seventeenth century, Catholics were just 1 to 5 percent of the overall population in England. In Maryland, they were nearly 10 percent of the population. See John Bossy, *The English Catholic Community, 1570-1850* (Oxford University Press: New York, 1976), Chapter 8; *Archives of Maryland*, William Hand Brown et al., ed., (Maryland Historical Society: Baltimore, 1883-present) 25:258-259.

[36] Thomas Jefferson, *Notes on the State of Virginia*, "Query XVII: Religion," 1781, *Teaching American History.org*, retrieved on October 25th, 2014 http://teachingamericanhistory.org/library/document/notes-on-the-state-of-virginia-query-xvii-religion/.

Cecilius Calvert, of course, had no intellectual influence on Thomas Jefferson. But John Locke—who is considered to be the "father" of religious toleration in the English-speaking world—did. And when we discover the roots of Locke's theory of toleration—and consider, then, that these were the roots that inspired people like Jefferson and his protégé, James Madison, the author of the First Amendment—it is then that we come to understand why the principle that animates America's constitutional approach to religion is one of "liberty," rather than "toleration."

The roots of Locke's theory of toleration can be found in his *Essay Concerning Human Understanding,* an inquiry into the limits of human knowledge that he published at roughly the same time as the *Letter Concerning Toleration.*[37] Toleration, for John Locke, is made necessary by one undeniable reality: when it comes to the existence of God and the nature of the proper relationship between God and humanity, we cannot know. Or rather, we *can* know, but we cannot know in a way that allows us to transmit our knowledge to even one other person.

As a political theorist, Locke was deeply concerned with the proper foundations for community formation. Knowledge that could not be shared—could not be spread easily and decisively throughout the community—was, for him, an improper and inherently unstable foundation for society. It is true that atheists were a source of concern for Locke, because "promises, covenants, and oaths, which are the bonds of human society, can have no hold on an atheist" (interestingly, this concern was not shared by Thomas Jefferson, who glibly told the Marquis de Barbé-Marbois that if the court testimony of an atheist "cannot be relied upon, reject it then, and be the stigma on

---

[37] For more on the link between the *Essay* and the theory of toleration that Locke puts forth in the Letter, see J. Judd Owen, "Locke's Case for Religious Toleration: Its Neglected Foundation in the Essay Concerning Human Understanding," *The Journal of Politics* 69, no. 1 (2007): 156-68; and Laurence D. Nee, "Lockean Rhetoric and Toleration: The Place of Language in the Thought of John Locke," Ph.D. dissertation, University of Dallas, 1998.

him").[38] But as a general rule, John Locke considered the answer to the God question to be beyond the pale of politics.

Locke was not as extreme as Cecilius Calvert when it came to the question of whether individuals were entitled to try to persuade others to adopt their religious beliefs. "Every man has commission to admonish, exhort, and convince another of error; and, by reasoning, to draw him into the truth," he writes in the *Letter*.[39] But if we examine this statement in light of what Locke says in the *Essay* about the ability of anyone to know what God is and what God expects from humanity, it seems highly unlikely that Locke viewed conversion as a productive activity—and he certainly did not see it as an appropriate one for the state.

This is because our understanding of God resides in what Locke calls the "intellectual world"—that is, the plane of ideas or the makings of the mind.[40] He does seem willing to allow that the existence of God can be known—fantastic claims by some scholars that Locke was a secret atheist aside.[41] Any knowledge we may have

---

[38] Locke, *A Letter Concerning Toleration*, 56; Jefferson, *Notes on the State of Virginia*, "Query XVII."

[39] Locke, ibid., 13.

[40] John Locke, *An Essay on Human Understanding* (1689), Book II, Chapter XII, rpt., Volume I (H. Woodfall, et al.: London, 1768), 124.

[41] Leo Strauss and a handful of prominent scholars who have been charmed by him contend that John Locke was actually an atheist who used the logic of his own arguments to secretly defend his spiritual skepticism for a small group of careful readers. Most historians of political thought, however, have rejected this idea. For a defense of Strauss's reading of Locke, see Michael Zuckert, *Launching Liberalism: On Lockean Political Philosophy* (Lawrence, Kansas: University of Kansas Press, 2002). For criticism of Strauss' reading, see Hans Aarsleff, "Some Observations on Recent Locke Scholarship" and Richard Ashcraft, "Faith and Knowledge in Locke's Philosophy," in John W. Yolton, ed. *John Locke: Problems and Perspectives* (Cambridge: New York, 1969), 262-272 and 194-223.

of God, however, is, of necessity, contained entirely within ourselves—what Locke calls an "obscure and relative" idea.[42]

The idea of "God," in other words, is personal and specific—as is the idea of a "horse," incidentally, according to John Locke. What makes the idea of a "horse" different from the idea of "God," however, is that the simple experiences an individual uses to construct the complex intellectual idea of a horse are experiences that can be had by everyone. They are, in that sense, experiences that can be shared – and the idea of a "horse," then, can consequently be learned, debated, and agreed upon by groups of people.

If a horse walked into a classroom full of suburban three-year-olds who had never encountered a farm animal before, each child in the room could experience its warmth, its smell, its furriness, its height, and its neigh to construct the idea of a "horse." The children would have to be taught by their teachers to do this, of course—and at the end of the day, the idea of a "horse" that one child has constructed on the basis of his experiences and learning may not be exactly the same as the idea that another child has constructed. This disparity could become important years later, if the children encountered another animal that neighed and was warm, smelly, and furry, but stood only eight hands high, instead of the traditional fifteen.[43]

But children can be taught by their teachers to construct the idea of a "horse"—and they can debate, then, whether a creature that smells, sounds, and feels like a horse, but is only three-and-a-half feet tall, is, in fact, a horse—because the experiences we all use to construct the idea of a "horse" are experiences that can be shared. Not so with the experiences we use to construct the complex intellectual idea of "God."

---

[42]John Locke, *An Essay on Human Understanding*, Book II, Chapter XXIII, 244, 247.

[43] Ibid., 246; Book II, Chapter XXVI, 279; Book II, Chapter XXVII, 282.

Our knowledge of the existence of God, according to Locke, comes from our knowledge of ourselves. What I experience is *me*—*my* thought, *my* desire, *my* pleasure, *my* pain. I take these experiences, then—which are available only to me and cannot, ultimately, be experienced by anyone else—and combine them with my reason to construct the idea of God.

I know, thanks to the experience of me, that I exist—that I am what Locke calls a "real being." And I also know—by means of "intuitive certainty," Locke says—that "bare nothing can no more produce any real being, than it can be equal to two right angles." I know that I am a real being because I have constructed the idea of myself as such from the experience of me. I apply my intuitive reason, then, to the idea of me as a real being, and I come to the conclusion that there must be an eternal and productive "something" that made me, because "nothing" cannot produce real beings.[44]

The idea of "God," then, is *the* most relative of Locke's "obscure and relative" ideas. It begins with me and relies entirely upon me. As such, it cannot be shared or taught—not even imprecisely, the way the idea of a "horse" can be. Our knowledge of God, therefore, is an inappropriate foundation for politics. I cannot share my knowledge with you, and you cannot share your knowledge with me. Even if my answer to the God question is "right," and yours is "wrong," I ought not to concern myself with your answer, because your answer will not touch mine, and my answer cannot touch yours.

To put it in Thomas Jefferson's words, "it does me no injury for my neighbor to say there are 20 gods or no god. It neither picks my pocket nor breaks my leg."[45]

\*\*\*

---

[44] John Locke, *An Essay on Human Understanding* (1689), Book IV, Chapter X, rpt., Volume II (A, Churchill, et al.: London, 1721), 239-240.

[45] Jefferson, *Notes on the State of Virginia*, "Query XVII: Religion."

This attitude that someone else's knowledge of God does me no injury is *not* toleration. Toleration hurts. It is painful for the Jewish granddaughter of a Holocaust survivor to tolerate another person as he says the Jews were complicit in their own persecution. It hurts the parents of a child who died at Sandy Hook Elementary School to tolerate another person as she insists that the government was behind the slaughter of their seven-year-old daughter. Toleration is, I suspect, what a lot of us engage in on an individual level, whenever we behave civilly toward someone whose beliefs are radically different from our own. But it is not what our constitution says we are about as a people.

Our constitution says that the "right" answer to the God question is essentially irrelevant. Our constitution does not find it painful to allow Muslims to worship a mile away from the World Trade Center site, or Catholics and Evangelicals to avoid paying for medical insurance that subsidizes I.U.D.s. Our constitution does not concern itself with whether there is a "right" answer to the God question, and if so, what that answer is. Our constitution is not about religious toleration; it is about religious liberty—a natural political byproduct of any philosophical foundation that says, as John Locke says, that a knowledge of God is unavoidably "obscure and relative."

# 4

## RELIGION AND SOCIAL UNITY: ANOTHER ROUSSEAUIAN PARADOX

### *Daniel Cullen*

The obligations of American citizens do not include obligations of faith; and yet, our laws nevertheless express a particular religious inheritance.[1] President Eisenhower was perhaps alluding to this complex relation of exclusion and cooperation between religion and politics when he famously remarked: "Our government makes no sense unless it is founded in a deeply felt religious faith—and I don't care what it is."[2] Robert Bellah boldly asserted that Americans have practiced what Jean-Jacques Rousseau called a "civil religion," by which he meant that they have habitually connected rather than

---

[1] "The American Bill of Rights is not a piece of eighteenth-century rationalist theory, it is far more the product of Christian history. Behind it one can see, not the philosophy of the Enlightenment but the older philosophy that had been the matrix of common law. The 'man' whose rights are guaranteed in the face of law and government is, whether he knows it or not, the Christian man, who had learned to know his own personal dignity in the school of Christian faith." John Courtney Murray, *We Hold These Truths: Catholic Reflections on the American Proposition* (New York: Shreed and Ward, 1960), 390, quoted in Michael Novak, "Free Persons and the Common Good" in *Liberty/Liberté* ed. Joseph Klaits and Michael H. Haltzel (Baltimore: Johns Hopkins University Press, 1991), 191.

[2] Dwight D. Eisenhower, in Will Herbert, *Protestant-Catholic-Jew* (Garden City, N.Y.: Doubleday and Co., 1955), 97. Cf. Alexis De Tocqueville, *Democracy in America*, trans. Harvey C. Mansfield and Delba Winthrop (Chicago: University of Chicago Press, 2000), Volume 1, Part 2, Chapter 9, 278: "If it serves man very much as an individual that his religion be true, this is not so for society. Society has nothing to fear nor hope from the other life; and what is most important to it is not so much that all citizens profess the true religion but that they profess a religion."

separated religious and political life, endowing the latter with a sacred dimension.³ But however characterized, this practice has generated difficult questions that require the clarifications of theory: Is religious freedom helped or hurt by the attempt to harmonize it with republican freedom? And what is to be done when the free exercise of religion collides with fundamental state concerns? The chief difficulty of specifying the nature and limits of religious freedom in modern democracy derives from the latter's reliance on secular principles of political legitimacy. When Americans discuss the place of religion in public life, they begin from the perspective of what reason permits rather than what faith prescribes.

The term "civil religion" denotes the informal ways in which privately held religious beliefs lend support to public institutions, a relation famously endorsed by Washington in his Farewell Address: "Of all the suppositions and habits which lead to political prosperity, religion and morality are indispensable supports. In vain would that man claim the tribute of patriotism, who should labor to subvert these great pillars of human happiness, these firmest props of the duties of men and citizens. The mere politician, equally with the pious man ought to respect and cherish them."⁴ In distinguishing "men and citizens," and in suggesting that duty required external reinforcement, Washington acknowledged (however inadvertently) a paradox that Rousseau's political philosophy made thematic: while modern civil life is not based on religion, it nevertheless requires it. Because

---

³ Robert N. Bellah, "Civil Religion in America" *Daedalus*, Winter 1967, Vol. 96, No. 1. For skeptical treatments of Bellah's thesis see: George Armstrong Kelly, *Politics and Religious Consciousness in America* New Brunswick, NJ: Transaction Publishers, 1984) and Bruce Frohnen, "Robert Bellah and the Politics of 'Civil' Religion," *The Political Science Reviewer*, Vol . 21 (Spring, 1992): 149-218.

⁴ Saxe Cummins, ed., *The Basic Writings of George Washington* (New York: Random House, 1948), 637. For a careful account of Washington's distinctive perspective on religion and political life and especially the dependence of good government on religious beliefs, see Phillip Munoz, *God and the Founders* (New York: Cambridge University Press, 2009), chapter 2.

legitimate government rests on consent, only will can obligate us; but citizens can only be tied together effectively by the force of religion.[5] According to Rousseau, the merely or strictly "political" man must respect a transcendent source of authority that cannot be accounted for by political reasoning alone; nevertheless, it must be emphasized that it is *reason* that discloses to us the necessity of religion in political life. This insight into the tension between the requirements of legitimacy and stability provides the armature around which Rousseau constructs his political thought, and in what follows I will argue that the issues of church-state separation, and religious freedom generally, can be illuminated by Rousseau's effort to think through the conflicting requirements of liberty and authority, freedom and obligation, which lie at the heart of democratic political life.[6]

John Witte's historical survey of separationist arguments underscores the Founders' desire to protect religious and political liberty from mutual antagonism.[7] The rhetoric of church-state separation typically appeals to the views expressed by John Locke in his influential *Letter Concerning Toleration*: that the Church has no rightful political authority; that it is a voluntary organization within civil society, dedicated to such public worship as its members agree upon; and that it may not dispense *civil* rewards or penalties. The state, for its part, is limited to assuring conformity of outward behavior rather than internal belief, leaving individuals to judge for themselves in matters of faith.[8]

---

[5] The etymology is instructive. The Latin *ligere* means to bind. See Roger Scruton, *The West and the Rest* (Wilmington: ISI Books, 2002), 1.

[6] On the character of Rousseau's political science see Hilail Gildin, *Rousseau's Social Contract: The Design of the Argument* (Chicago: University of Chicago Press, 1983). See also Roger D. Masters, *The Political Philosophy of Rousseau* (Princeton: Princeton University Press, 1986).

[7] John Witte Jr., "The Shifting Walls of Separation Between Church and State in the United States," in this volume.

[8] John Locke, *A Letter Concerning Toleration*, ed. James Tully (Indianapolis: Hackett Publishing, 1983).

The division of authority implied by the notion of church-state separation is familiar to Americans, but we might linger over the verbs "divide" and "separate," which mean to "force apart." The very terms seem to presuppose an original unity, or a tendency toward unity, one that is subsequently ruptured or interfered with. Attention to the disruptive connotation of the church-state trope reminds us that an argument in favor of separation has to be made, and that separationist rhetoric (as Witte describes it), with its invocation of "two cities," "two swords," etc., might indicate a problem as much as a solution, given that religion naturally exerts authority over the whole of life. The continuing challenge of American democracy has been to simultaneously guarantee freedom *of*, *for*, and *from* religion for a people whose secular political principles both do and do not rely on a transcendent source.[9]

As the recent case of *Burwell v. Hobby Lobby Stores* demonstrates, citizens can be expected to challenge the propriety of their government deciding what is and what is not religious conduct. Religious life appears to be a whole resistant to compartmentalization, or to confinement to the private sphere. The government's argument in the *Hobby Lobby* case suggested that when religious people engage in commerce they in effect abstract themselves from their religious identity in favor of their corporate personality, and as a consequence forfeit their right to religious expression.[10] But a careful

---

[9] The Declaration of Independence appeals to reason rather than faith and stresses natural rights rather than duties to the Creator; but the Declaration also traces those rights to a transcendent source and appeals to the continuing protection of divine providence. Interestingly, the Constitution makes no mention either of God (or, for that matter, natural rights) which perhaps explains Madison's acute concern (in *Federalist* 49) for instilling a popular attitude of reverence. On the sacred and secular dimensions of the Declaration and the Constitution, see David Lowenthal, *Present Dangers: Rediscovering the First Amendment* (Dallas: Spence Publishing, 2002), 208-9.

[10] In a 5-4 decision the Supreme Court ruled that a mandate required by the U.S. Department of Health and Human Services to provide certain

reading of the historical record shows that the Founders understood religion to extend beyond private belief into the activities of ordinary life, including commerce.[11] Apart from the precise constitutional questions in *Hobby Lobby*, the case reminds us of a significant feature of religious identity: to be an "individual" is to be incapable of being *divided*. Stated differently, the integrity of religious belief connotes an experience of unity or wholeness that is at odds with a facile notion of church-state separation.

Rousseau's entire philosophical anthropology is enucleated in this notion of escaping the experience of division by being oneself, being a properly self-centered whole.[12] The disunity of the individual is, by contrast, assumed by the premises of the liberal democratic political model which requires actors in the public realm to justify their claims by "public reasons," omitting many things that might move the private conscience. So it is that we experience a constant struggle over "the scope of freedom for religious expression and worship, and the appropriateness of exemptions from ordinary rules for those with objections based on religious conscience."[13] According to an influential contemporary account, liberal democracy requires not merely that the justification of our political institutions be secular but that government remain neutral on the question of the best way of life.[14] The obligation to obey is thus divorced from any and all

---

contraceptive services to its employees through the company's health insurance plan substantially burdened the religious beliefs of Hobby Lobby's owners in violation of the Religious Freedom Restoration Act.

[11] Michael W. McConnell, "The Origins and Historical Understanding of Free Exercise of Religion," 103 *Harvard Law Review* (1990).

[12] On the importance of natural unity in Rousseau's thought, see Arthur Melzer, *The Natural Goodness of Man* (Chicago: University of Chicago Press, 1990).

[13] Kent Greenawalt, *Religious Convictions and Political Life* (Oxford: Oxford University Press, 1988), 7.

[14] Ronald Dworkin, "Liberalism" in *A Matter of Principle* (Cambridge: Harvard University Press, 1985).

intimations of the sacred and the onus falls on the pious individual to respect mere political or "public" reason. According to current liberal theory, religious convictions are no longer an acceptable foundation for public decisions.[15] Although our constitutional principles and political practice do not simply reflect the new principles of liberal neutrality, we have migrated considerably from Washington's assumption that a civil society founded on the rights of man requires the support of religion.[16]

Whether this movement away from traditional American assumptions of the interdependence of religious and political freedom represents progress or decline remains at issue in our on-going culture war.[17] One side reasons that insofar as morality depends on religion, and republican government requires civic virtue, government might promote religion generally, without violating the freedom of non-believers or offending the conscientious beliefs of different sects. It follows that "separationism" should not be interpreted to disqualify the religious citizen from civic activity. The other side, deeming religion incapable of neutral treatment, would require "citizens of faith" to "translate" their religious language into terms acceptable to public reason if they are to play a civic role.[18] Rousseau would be sympathetic to the former view, which emphasizes the utility of

---

[15] On "public reason" see John Rawls, *Political Liberalism*, (New York: Columbia University Press, 1996).

[16] Walter Berns, "Religion and the Founding Principle" in Robert H. Horwitz ed., *The Moral Foundations of the American Republic*, 3rd edition (Charlottesville: University Press of Virginia, 1986), 213. Berns argues for a widespread agreement among the Founders to the effect that while the American regime was emphatically not founded on a religious truth, the principles of free government required the support of religious belief, and that religious belief could be absolutely free because it was a means rather than the end of good government. Ibid., 228.

[17] James Davison Hunter, *Culture Wars: The Struggle to Define America* (New York: Basic Books, 1993).

[18] See Jurgen Habermas, *Between Naturalism and Religion* (Cambridge: Polity Press, 2008), 131-32.

religion rather than its truth, and aims at good citizenship rather than doctrinal conformity. But insofar as he believed the natural tendency of religion is to weaken strictly political norms, Rousseau shares the "public reason" concern that "the fundamentals of political life should be more or less agreed upon and set outside ordinary political wrangling."[19]

Rousseau distinguished his own view from that of his contemporaries, Bayle and Warburton, who asserted respectively that "no Religion is useful to the body politic" and, contrarily, that "Christianity is its firmest support." Against the first position, Rousseau declared that "a State has never been founded without Religion serving as its base;" but he stopped short of endorsing complete religious freedom and, in opposition to the second position, concluded that the emergence of Christianity created a new problem of divided loyalty.[20] Because it takes seriously the arguments in favor of both separation and unity, Rousseau's account of the relation of religious convictions and political principles merits reconsideration. His conception of religious citizenship or civil religion is indeed paradoxical, but only because it comes to grips (or at least so Rousseau would insist) with the contradictions in the nature of modern democracy.

As noted above, Rousseau's thought as a whole responds to the human predicament stemming from the loss of our original unity. "What causes human misery is the contradiction between our condition and our desires, between our duties and our inclinations, between nature and social institutions, between the man and the citizen. Make man united (*render l'homme un*) and you will make him as happy as he can be. Give him entirely to the state or leave him

---

[19] Kent Greenawalt, *Private Consciences and Public Reasons* (New York: Oxford University Press, 1995), 106.

[20] Jean-Jacques Rousseau, *Social Contract* IV.8.14. (Hereafter cited SC, followed by book, chapter and paragraph number.) Unless otherwise indicated, translations from the Social Contract are from *The Collected Writings of Rousseau*, Volume 4, eds. Roger Masters and Christopher Kelly (Hanover: University Press of New England, 1994).

entirely to himself; but if you divide his heart you tear him to pieces."[21] Let the individual be either "man" or "citizen," let him live according to nature or according to convention ("political right," in Rousseau's terminology). In principle there should be no gap between the realms of natural right and political right, for human beings cannot live, as it were, with one foot in and one foot out of the state of nature without jeopardizing the conventional order. Rousseau's writings imagine a variety of ways our original unity of soul might be restored in new and unnatural conditions.[22] But different ways of life entail different kinds of souls; and being a "citizen" and being a "man" represent incompatible alternatives.[23] Viewed in this light, the prospect of being a "religious citizen" is deeply problematical. Which city will one serve: God's or man's?

Rousseau's discussion of civil religion proper is governed by the same concern for psychic unity, treated now from an explicitly political perspective: "Everything that destroys social unity is worthless. All institutions that put man in contradiction with himself are worthless."[24] In a brief excursus on religion and politics, Rousseau emphasizes that originally the two were indistinguishable.[25] The first peoples understood their rulers to be their gods, and wars between

---

[21] "On Public Happiness," *Collected Writings*, 41. Quotations from the French text are to Jean-Jacques Rousseau, *Oeuvres complètes*, Bernard Gagnebin et Marcel Raymond eds. (Paris: Pléiade, 1959-), Volume III, 510.

[22] I examine Rousseau's attempt at a political solution to the human problem in *Freedom in Rousseau's Political Philosophy* (DeKalb: Northern Illinois University Press, 1993).

[23] Victor Gourevitch, "Introduction," *Rousseau: The Social Contract and Other Later Political Writings* (Cambridge: Cambridge University Press, 1997), xxix-xxx.

[24] SC IV.8.17.

[25] This paragraph draws on Gildin, *Rousseau's Social Contract*, 181 ff. See also, Ronald Beiner, "Machiavelli, Hobbes, and Rousseau on Civil Religion," *The Review of Politics*, Vol. 55, No.4 (Autumn, 1993): 617-638; Charles M. Sherover, "Rousseau's Civil Religion," *Interpretation*, Vol. 8, No.2-3 (May, 1980): 114-122.

peoples were consequently viewed as wars between gods. The inseparability of religion and politics was preserved when Rome achieved universal dominance, but Christianity's triumph over Rome disrupted the rapprochement between sacred and secular authorities. By introducing the notion of a spiritual kingdom, Christianity undermined the social spirit (*l'esprit social*) or national identity on which political life depends. The conundrum of *modern* politics is that the principles of political right enshrined by the social contract are in actuality the expression rather than the cause of this social spirit.[26] The need for civil religion thus arises from the requirements of social unity that, in Rousseau's judgment, rational principles alone cannot satisfy.

Viewed sociologically, three types of religion can be distinguished. The "religion of man" corresponds to the most general or universal society and Rousseau associates it with an undogmatic or "pure" Christianity and with a generic theism. The "religion of the citizen" is, by contrast, exclusively national, and its dogmas are prescribed by the laws. The "religion of the priest" generates divided loyalties that make it impossible to be either a devout man or a good citizen.[27] From a *political* perspective, each religious type has its characteristic defect. Without temples, altars and rites, the religion of man is a "purely interior" [as contrasted with "purely civil" or exterior] belief that encourages a humanitarian virtue so universal as to breed political indifference. The religion of the citizen conflates the love of God with the love of the laws and stimulates an intolerant and

---

[26] "In order for an emerging people to appreciate the healthy maxims of politics…the effect would have to become the cause; the social spirit, which should be the result of the institution [of the social order], would have to preside over the founding of the institution itself; and men would have to be prior to the laws what they ought to become by means of the laws." SC II.7.9. Robert Derathé notes that Rousseau drafted his chapter on civil religion on the verso side of his chapter on the Legislator, indicating that he regarded their arguments as complementary. *Oeuvres Complètes* III, 1498, n.1.

[27] SC IV.8. 15-16.

unreflective zeal. The religion of the priest, exemplified by Roman Catholicism, inevitably usurps political authority and is, in Rousseau's judgment, essentially incompatible with social unity.[28]

Given the importance he attributes to social solidarity, one might expect Rousseau to subordinate religious belief to political considerations in the manner of the religion of the citizen; but he rejects the latter as false, violent and inhumane. Having considered religion from a sociological and political point of view, Rousseau turns to religion viewed from the perspective of political right (*droit*) and from this vantage point considers the case for "*une profession de foi purement civile*," a profession of a purely civil or purely political faith.[29] As is so often the case with Rousseau, what seems to be a confusing or contradictory formulation highlights a genuine difficulty in the nature of things. Simply put, the law's legitimacy can only arise from the consent of the people subject to it, but if the law is not sanctified, that is, regarded as transcending the people, it will lack moral force and practical efficacy. And it is here, I suggest, that Rousseau's precise effort to integrate the sacred and the secular without deforming either sheds important light on the continuing struggle between "conservative liberals," who view free government as depending on a reservoir of moral capital, and "neutralist liberals," who would exclude from the domain of public reason all views that express a substantive morality.

As we have seen, Rousseau agrees with the contemporary liberal view that the justification of political institutions must rest on non-religious foundations, but he points up a conundrum of secular democracy. The social contract is the exclusively legitimate foundation of society, which is to say that the individual will is its true or ultimate foundation. But social unity cannot effectively be preserved on this rationalist and voluntarist basis alone. It is to *this* problem that Rousseau proposes civil religion as the solution. The social tie (*lien*

---

[28] Cf. Tocqueville's argument that "Catholics in the United States are at once the most submissive of the faithful and the most independent of citizens." *Democracy in America*, 277.

[29] SC IV.8.32.

*social*) must be sanctified precisely because its origin is the will of the individual rather than the will of God. Although society cannot legitimately be founded on religion, the latter is indispensable to its preservation. The political order that is established by the concurrence of individual wills, and then realized and legitimated by the general will, must be consecrated in order to have effective authority. If citizens regard nothing transcending their own sovereignty they will be disinclined, over the long run, to respect their own political creations. Thus, while religion is not the source of freedom, it encourages those habits of the heart (as Tocqueville called them) that permit a people to *remain* free. The conscientious citizen, through a self-imposed *tromp l'oeil*, will come to regard the social order as sacred rather than an object of self-serving choice. Civil religion properly understood has an unimpeachably secular purpose; its articles of faith are not religious dogmas but "sentiments of sociability," by which Rousseau means nothing more than the disposition to be just and law-abiding according to the terms of the social contract that makes social membership possible in the first place. Civil religion may thus be said to routinize the charisma of the quasi-divine Legislator who creates the social spirit on which the efficacy of political institutions depend, but which cannot be accounted for by the rational agreement that establishes those institutions.

The complications of Rousseau's analysis are attributable to his recognition that liberal politics requires a conservative foundation. The fact that we must have an ordered social life for human freedom to flourish arguably gives the maintenance of that order primacy over the matter of consent. Because the 'social spirit" on which political life depends cannot be nurtured by abstract political principles (*droit politique*), citizens must regard their common political identity as sacred. As we have seen, Rousseau takes pains to emphasize that the so-called dogmas of civil religion are not really beliefs at all but an expression of a basic loyalty without which it is impossible to regard oneself as a member of a larger whole.[30] In their *civil* aspect, these

---

[30] SC IV.8.32.

beliefs are feelings (*sentiments*) that reinforce secular conceptions of justice; but as an expression of *faith* those feelings are a necessary token of the sincerity of one's commitment to otherwise religiously-neutral obligations In response to a critic, Rousseau summarized his complicated teaching as follows: "In society, everyone has the right to find out whether another person *believes* himself obligated to be just, and the Sovereign has the right to examine the reasons on which each person bases this obligation."[31] Two background assumptions merit mention: the first is that rational principles of justice do not compel attachment, which explains why a religious commitment, however formal or cursory, remains an indispensable guarantee of social trust; the second is that the sovereign's attention to such warrants reflects the primacy of public reason. Belief itself is beyond the sovereign's purview, and while the recalcitrant citizen might indeed be punished, it will not be for impiety but rather for being "unsociable" (*insociable*) in the sense of refusing to obey rationally valid laws.[32]

Rousseauian civil religion properly understood has nothing to do with enforcing conformity of religious belief; it has everything to do with maintaining the social spirit that is indispensable to political justice. Moral behavior depends on a religious motive, but it is the moral consequence that matters to Rousseau, not the motivating belief. The civil "profession of faith" aims only at cultivating a disposition of law-abidingness. What distinguishes Rousseau from the proponents of liberal neutrality is his attention to its affective

---

[31] Rousseau, "Letter to Beaumont" in *Rousseau on Philosophy, Morality and Religion*, ed. Christopher Kelly (Hanover, NH: Dartmouth College Press, 2007), 199. Emphasis added.

[32] This is the plain meaning of Rousseau's rhetorical flourish: "If someone who has publicly acknowledged these same dogmas behaves as though he does not believe them, he should be punished with death. He has committed the greatest of crimes: he lied before the laws." SC IV.8. 33.

conditions, to the sense of committed *membership* that is nurtured, perhaps exclusively, by religious feeling.[33]

Like so much else in Rousseau's thought, the argument for civil religion culminates in a paradox: the citizen must believe and the sovereign must not compel belief. But why must citizens believe in an authority that transcends their own united will? It seemed to Rousseau to be a sociological fact that human beings will not take their obligations seriously if they do not regard them as sacred. And yet, civil religion does not determine the whole of life, and the sovereign power does not exceed the limits of public utility.[34] In his own way, Rousseau arrives at the distinction, familiar to us, between the public and the private, the politically relevant and the politically indifferent spheres. The fundamental question is whether a person's religious views can be considered a wholly private matter, a conclusion that Rousseau (along with Locke, and the American Founders) rejects. Rousseau draws brief yet fine distinctions between duty and dogma, action and belief. The sovereign has a legitimate concern that citizens respect their duties and only cares about respecting dogmas insofar as they bear on those duties. "[A]s for opinions that are not connected to morality, that do not influence actions in any way, and that do not tend to transgress Laws," Rousseau concludes that each has the right to his own judgment.[35] In this regard, Rousseau's view seems to be in accord with the axioms of liberal political philosophy: the basis of civil obligation must be secular, and religious belief must not seek expression in law.

But there are also non-liberal lessons to draw from Rousseau's reflections on civil religion. One is that authority might serve freedom rather than undermine it. Another is that the freedom of conscience that we rightly prize is an expression of our natural existence which

---

[33] Cf. Roger Scruton, *A Political Philosophy: Arguments for Conservatism* (London: continuum, 2006), 14: "People need to identify themselves through a first-person plural if they are to accept the sacrifices required by society."

[34] SC IV.8.31; cf. II.4.4.

[35] "Letter to Beaumont," 199.

remains in permanent tension with our existence *qua* citizens. Because political association confers only an artificial identity, political obligation requires moral supports, including religious belief. For the social tie to be effective it must be viewed as a transcendent bond that cannot be conceived as an object of contractual choice. Thus far Rousseau's argument is in tune with that of conservative liberals who acknowledge the need for foundations beyond what human wills can reliably authorize. But it is a small step from acknowledging a transcendent bond to acknowledging a divine will as its source, at which point the free play of religious convictions can invite intolerance.

Rousseau's reflections on the theological-political problem leaves us grappling with a puzzle: religion is and is not the foundation of society depending on whether one's perspective is historical and empirical or "moral" which, in Rousseau's distinctive usage, pertains to relations construed on the plane of "right" rather than either nature or history.[36] Rousseau was fully aware that the general will was a moral or artificial conception rather than a natural feeling, and he was under no illusions about its effectiveness. As we have seen, Rousseau's civil religion does not aim beyond instilling the habit of law-abidingness. The challenge facing Rousseau was to draw on religious motives for the sake of their moral effects without restoring religion as an independent authority. But he rejected in advance the notion that one might supply the defect of religious motives by neutral reason alone. To the extent that modern institutions have lost their purchase on the allegiance of citizens at the same time as sectarian challenges to public authority increase, the predicament of a purely secular politics is evident.[37] The challenge facing conservative and neutralist liberals alike is to manage the tension Rousseau discovered in the conflicting imperatives of modern democracy.

---

[36] On Rousseau's precise conception of "moral personality," see Robert Derathé, *Jean-Jacques Rousseau et la Science Politique de Son Temps* (Paris: Presses Universitaires de France, 1950), 397-413.

[37] See Kelly, *Politics and Religious Consciousness*, 32.

PART II

RELIGIOUS LIBERTY AND THE AMERICAN FOUNDING

# 5

## THE SHIFTING WALLS OF SEPARATION BETWEEN CHURCH AND STATE IN THE UNITED STATES

*John Witte, Jr.*

The civic catechisms and canticles of our day still celebrate Thomas Jefferson's experiment in religious liberty. To end a millennium of repressive religious establishments, we are taught, Jefferson sought liberty in the twin formulas of privatizing religion and secularizing politics. Religion must be "a concern purely between our God and our consciences," he wrote in 1802. Politics must be conducted with "a wall of separation between church and state."[1] Public religion is a threat to private religion, and must thus be discouraged. Political ministry is a menace to political integrity and must thus be outlawed.

These Jeffersonian maxims remain for many today the cardinal axioms of a unique American logic of religious freedom to which every patriotic individual and institution should yield. Every public school student learns the virtues of keeping his Bible at home and her prayers in the closet. Every church knows the tax law advantages of high cultural conformity and low political temperature. Every politician understands the calculus of courting religious favors without subvening religious causes. Religious privatization is the bargain we must strike to attain religious freedom for all. A high and impregnable wall of separation is the barrier we must build to contain religious bigotry for good.

"A page of history is worth a volume of logic," Oliver Wendell Holmes, Jr. once said. And careful historical work in the past three decades has begun to call a good deal of this popular Jeffersonian

---

[1] H. Washington, ed., *The Writings of Thomas Jefferson*, 10 vols. (Washington, DC: Taylor and Maury, 1853-1854), 8:113.

logic into question. Jefferson's views on the separation of church and state are considerably more nuanced than this simple wall metaphor would have us believe. The fuller account now available of the genesis and exodus of the American experiment in religious liberty suggests that separation of church and state is only one principle of religious freedom in American law, and it is balanced by other founding principles of religious freedom—liberty of conscience, freedom of exercise, religious pluralism, religious equality, and no establishment of religion.

In this brief essay, I analyse five distinct understandings of separation of church and state at work in the American founding era of 1776-1812 when the federal and first state constitutional guarantees of religious freedom were drafted and ratified. I sketch briefly the continued influence and manifestations of each of these five understandings in current American constitutional law. The last section argues that separation of church and state is a valuable constitutional ideal, so long as it used prudentially not categorically, and so long as it remains balanced with other founding principles of religious freedom.[2]

## Separation of Church from State

First, the eighteenth-century American founders used the idea of separation to protect the church from the state. This had been a common Christian understanding of separation of church and state from the beginning, and it was captured in the Christian clergy's perennial call for "freedom of the church"—or what the Edict of Milan of 313 had called the "free exercise and practice of religious groups."[3] This understanding of separation of church and state was

---

[2] This article draws in part from John Witte, Jr. and Joel A. Nichols, *Religion and the American Constitutional Experiment*, 3d ed. (Boulder, CO: Westview Press, 2011), which includes detailed citations. Hereafter noted as "RCE".

[3] In Lactantius, *De Mortibus Persecutorum* [c. 315], 48.2-12, ed. and trans. J. L. Creed (Cambridge: Cambridge University Press, 1984), 71–73.

prominent in eighteenth-century America, and remains so to this day. The founders' principal concern was to protect church affairs from state intrusion, the clergy from the magistracy, church properties and polities from state interference, ecclesiastical rules and rites from political coercion and control. George Washington wrote in 1785 of the need "to establish effectual barriers" so that there was no threat "to the religious rights of any ecclesiastical Society," including particularly beleaguered minorities like Jews, Catholics, and Quakers, to whom he wrote several tender letters.[4] Thomas Jefferson called for government to resist what he called "intermeddling with religious institutions, their doctrines, discipline, or exercises." "Every religious society has a right to determine for itself the times for these exercises, & the objects proper for them, according to their own peculiar tenets," Jefferson wrote. And none of this can "concern or involve" the state.[5]

This first understanding of separation was captured especially in early American state constitutional guarantees of the free exercise rights of peaceable religious groups—the right of religious bodies to incorporate and to hold property, to appoint and remove clergy and other officials, to have sites and rites of worship, education, charity, mission, and burial, to maintain standards of entrance and exit for their members, and more—all of which were specified in early state constitutional laws.[6] This understanding of separation was also implicit in the First Amendment guarantee that government was not to establish religion but to leave religion to the free exercise of individuals and groups.

---

[4] Using critical version in Daniel L. Dreisbach, *Thomas Jefferson and the Wall of Separation Beween Church and State* (New York: NYU Press, 2002), 84-85.

[5] Thomas Jefferson, Letter to Rev. Samuel Miller (1808), in *The Founders' Constitution*, ed. Philip Kurland and Ralph S. Lerner, 5 vols. (Chicago: University of Chicago Press, 1987), 5:98–99.

[6] See esp. Chester J. Antieau, Phillip Mark Carroll and Thomas Carroll Burke, *Religion Under the State Constitutions* (Brooklyn: Central Book Co., 1965).

This first understanding of separation of church and state has long been a vital part of American constitutional law. In more than 20 cases from 1872 to 2012, the United States Supreme Court has held that religious organizations have the right to organize their own internal religious affairs without state interference, to resolve their own internal disputes without judicial intrusion, and to hire and fire employees who do not share their religious vision.[7] Today, the exact edges of these "corporate free exercise rights" or claims to "church autonomy" are being closely tested. Are secular organizations run by sincere religious individuals—say a hardware or hobby store, run by a Catholic businessman—deserving of religious freedom protection? Are services like schooling, charity, or emergency relief deserving of special religious freedom protection, when secular organizations offer comparable services? Is every activity of a religious organization—say its decisions about hiring a janitor or ordering paper for the Sunday bulletin—protected by religious freedom norms? These and other hard new questions of application, however, do not change the reality that religious organizations are presumptively protected from the state.

## Separation of State from Church

Second, the American founders invoked the principle of separation to protect the state from the church. This was largely a post-Westphalian concern in Western Europe, but it became prominent among some American founders, too. "The sorest tyrannies have been those, who have united the royalty and priesthood in one person," wrote the authors of *Cato's Letters*. "Churchmen when they ruled states, had not only double authority but also double insolence and remarkably less mercy and regard to conscience, property," and the

---

[7] See cases in RCE, 241-62 and most recently *Hosanna-Tabor Evangelical Lutheran Church and School v. Equal Employment Opportunity Commission*, 132 S. Ct. 694 (2012).

domains and demands of statecraft.[8] In the same vein, John Adams documented at length what he called the "tyrannous outrages" that the medieval Catholic Church and early modern Protestant churches had inflicted through their control of the state. Adams called this "a wicked confederacy between two systems of tyranny."[9] Drawing on these same historical lessons, John Jay urged his fellow constitutional conveners in New York "not only to expel civil tyranny, but also to guard against that spiritual oppression and intolerance wherewith the bigotry and ambition of weak and wicked priests and princes have scourged mankind."[10]

This understanding of separation helped to inform the movement in some states to exclude ministers and other religious officials from participating in political office. Ministers in political office, it was commonly argued, could use the threat of spiritual reprisal to force their congregants, including fellow politicians who sat in their pews, to acquiesce in their political positions. Ministers could be conflicted over whose interests to represent and serve—the interests of their religious congregants or their political constituents. Ministers could have disproportionate influence on the political process since they represented both religious congregants and political constituents. Ministers who tried to serve both God and the state could be distracted from their fundamental callings of preaching and teaching, and tempted to train their religious messages toward political causes. Ministers could not enjoy both the benefit of exemption of taxation for themselves and the power to impose

---

[8] John Trenchard and Thomas Gordon, *Cato's Letters, or Essays on Liberty, Civil and Religious, and Other Important Subjects*, [1720-23], 2 vols., ed. Ronald Hamowy (Indianapolis: Liberty Fund Press, 1995), 2:467-468.

[9] *The Works of John Adams,* ed. J.F. Adams, 10 vols. (Boston: Little Brown, 1850-56), 3:447.

[10] New York Constitution (1777), Arts. XXXVIII-XXXIX.

taxation on all others; this was even more odious than the great offense of taxation without representation.[11]

These kinds of arguments led seven of the original thirteen states, and fifteen later states, to ban ministers from serving in political office.[12] In 1978, the Supreme Court struck down these per se prohibitions on clerical participation in politics.[13] And in 1983, the Court upheld the long tradition of having chaplains serve in state legislatures—and in the military, in state prisons, in public hospitals, asylums, and other state-run service organizations.[14] But the custom of keeping clergy out of daily politics and keeping overt religious arguments out of political deliberations has remained strong. Federal tax and bankruptcy laws still require that tax exempt religious organizations refrain from direct participation in political elections or clear endorsement of one political party or candidate.

## Separation and Freedom of Conscience

Third, the American founders sometimes invoked the principle of separation of church and state as a means to protect the individual's liberty of conscience from the intrusions of either church or state, or both conspiring together. James Madison put this case in his famous 1785 "Memorial and Remonstrance Against Religious Assessments," calling for what he called "a great barrier" between church and state to defend the religious rights of the individual. Thomas Jefferson's equally famous 1802 letter to the Danbury Baptist Association also tied the principle of separation of church and state directly to the

---

[11] See sources in John Witte, Jr., "'A Most Mild and Equitable Establishment of Religion': John Adams and the 1780 Massachusetts Constitution," *Journal of Church and State* 41(1999): 242ff.

[12] Daniel L. Dreisbach, "The Constitution's Forgotten Religion Clause: Reflections on the Article VI Religious Test Ban," *Journal of Church and State* 38 (1996): 261-295.

[13] *McDaniel v. Paty*, 435 U.S. 618 (1978).

[14] *Marsh v. Chambers*, 463 U.S. 783 (1983).

principle of liberty of conscience. After his opening salutation, Jefferson's letter reads thus:

> Believing with you that *religion is a matter which lies solely between a man and his God,* that he owes account to none other for his faith or his worship, that the [legitimate] powers of government reach actions only, and not opinions, I contemplate with sovereign reverence that act of the whole American people which declared that their legislature should "make no law respecting an establishment of religion, or prohibiting the free exercise thereof," *thus building a wall of separation between church and State.* Adhering to this expression of the supreme will of the nation *in behalf of the rights of conscience,* I shall see with sincere satisfaction the progress of those sentiments which tend to *restore to man all his natural rights,* convinced he has no natural right in opposition to his social duties.[15]

In Jefferson's formulation here, separation of church and state assured individuals of their natural right of conscience, which could be exercised freely and fully to the point of breaching or shirking social duties.

This idea of separation remains strong today in modern American constitutional laws that protect parties from coerced participation in religious activities or associations that they find odious: so public school teachers cannot require their students to participate in prayers, Bible reading, or worship. Military or prison chaplains cannot force their soldiers or prisoners to attend religious worship services. Government officials cannot be required to swear a religious oath as a condition for office, nor may courts require a party or witness to swear an oath as a condition of their appearance or testimony. For the government to coerce religious exercises, the Court has repeatedly said, violates both the liberty of conscience of the coerced party and the limitation on government action imposed by the separation principle.[16]

---

[15] In Dreisbach, *Thomas Jefferson,* 148 (emphasis added).
[16] See cases in RCE, 191-98, 223-36.

## Separation and Federalism

Fourth, the American founders occasionally used the principle of separation of church and state to argue for the protection of the individual states from interference by the federal government in governing local religious affairs. Jefferson pressed this federalist jurisdictional sense of separation as well. He said many times that the federal government had no jurisdiction over religion; religion was entirely a state and local matter in his view. As he put it in his Second Inaugural Address as President: "In matters of religion, I have considered that its free exercise is placed by the constitution independent of the [federal] government. I have therefore undertaken, on no occasion, to prescribe the religious exercises suited to it; but have left them, as the constitution found them, under the direction and discipline of State or Church authorities."[17] The separation that Jefferson had in mind here was between local church-state relations and the federal government. The federal government could not interfere in the affairs of local churches, and the federal government could not interfere in the affairs of states in their governance of local churches. Under this federalist jurisdictional reading of separationism, state governments were free to patronize and protect religion, or to prohibit or abridge religion, as their own state constitutions dictated. But the federal government was entirely foreclosed from the same and from interference.

Some scholars have imputed this fourth understanding of separation of church and state into the First Amendment provision that "Congress shall make no law *respecting* an establishment of religion." The argument is that Congress shall make no laws respecting any *state establishment* of religion. In 1789, when the First Amendment was being drafted, seven of the original thirteen states still had some form of religious establishment, which both their state legislatures and constitutional conventions defined and defended, often against strong opposition. Moreover, Virginia had just passed

---

[17] Quoted in Dreisbach, *Thomas Jefferson*, 152.

Jefferson's bill for the "*establishment* of religious freedom," also against firm opposition. Having just defended their state establishments (of whatever sort) at home, the new members of Congress were not about to relinquish control of them to the new federal government.

This federalist reading of the establishment clause is becoming more prominent in the literature today, especially as neo-federalist movements have emerged in other areas of American constitutional law. This reading has recently captured the imagination of Justice Clarence Thomas of the Supreme Court who several times has called for the Court to abstain from First Amendment review of state and local government action.[18] This reading has also encouraged states' rights activists to push for the development of new state and local laws on religious freedom, some more permissive, some less permissive than allowed under the First Amendment.

## Separation of Religion from Political and Public Life

Fifth, a few of the American founders invoked the principle of separation to call for the separation of religion from public life altogether. Already before the American Revolution of 1776, several religious groups used separation of church and state language to argue against the established church policies of mandatory payments of tithes, required participation in swearing oaths, forced attendance at religious services, compulsory registration of church properties and more. At the turn of the nineteenth century, the language of separation of church and state also began to fuel broader campaigns for a much stricter separation of religion from political and public life altogether.

These new strict separationists taught that the state should not give special aid, support, privilege, or protection to religious doctrines or groups—through special tax appropriations or collections of tithes, special donations of goods and realty, special laws of religious

---

[18] See, e.g., *Elk Grove Unified School District v. Newdow*, 542 U.S. 1, 46 (2004) (Thomas J. concurring); *Zelman v. Simmons-Harris*, 536 U.S. 639-677-680 (2002) (Thomas J. concurring).

incorporation, or special criminal laws against blasphemy, sacrilege, and Sabbath-breaking. The state should not predicate its laws on explicitly religious premises or direct them to exclusively religious purposes. The state should not draw on the services of religious officials to discharge its political tasks, nor interfere in the order, organization, or orthodoxy of religious bodies. As James Madison put it in 1822: "[A] perfect separation between ecclesiastical and civil matters" is the best course, for "religion and Government will both exist in greater purity, the less they are mixed together."[19]

This was the most novel, and most controversial, understanding of separation of church and state in the young American republic. But it began to gain traction in the series of nineteenth-century battles over duelling, freemasonry, lotteries, drunkenness, Sunday laws, slavery, marriage, divorce, women's property rights, women's suffrage, religious education, blasphemy prosecutions, enforcement of Christian morals, and more. These were battles fought in Congress and in the courts, in states and on the frontier, in churches and in the schools, in clubs and at the ballot box. They were largely wars of words, occasionally wars of arms. The battles included many familiar foes—Republicans and Federalists, Catholics and Protestants, the north and the south, native Americans and new emigrants. They also included a host of newly established political groups: the Know-Nothing Party, the American Protective Association, the National Liberal League, the American Secular Union, the Ku Klux Klan, and dozens of other new groups.[20]

The largest battles over the meaning and means of separating church and state erupted over religious education and state funding. Thirty-five state constitutions ultimately prohibited state funding of

---

[19] Letter to Edward Livingston (July 10, 1820), in *The Writings of James Madison*, ed. G. Hunt, 9 vols. (New York: G.P. Putnam's Sons, 1900-1910), 9:98, 102.

[20] See articles collected in T. Jeremy Gunn and John Witte, Jr., *No Establishment of Religion: America's Original Contribution to Religious Liberty* (New York: Oxford University Press, 2012), 180-340.

religious schools. Fifteen state constitutions further insisted that state schools remain free from "sectarian influence" or from the control of religious officials and institutions. These provisions were motivated, in no small part, by growing Protestant biases against emerging Catholic schools. In the later nineteenth and early twentieth centuries, twenty-nine state constitutions broadened their rule of no-state-funding-for-religion to apply not only to religious schools but to all religious causes and institutions.[21]

It was this fifth version of strict separation of church and state logic that the Supreme Court highlighted in its landmark case of *Everson v. Board of Education* (1947). This case made two major moves at once. First, the Court applied the First Amendment establishment clause for the first time to federal, state, and local government alike—creating a uniform religious freedom law for the nation. Second, Justice Black read a strict separationist understanding into this First Amendment establishment clause:

> Neither a state nor the Federal Government can set up a church. Neither can pass laws which aid one religion, aid all religions, or prefer one religion over another.... No tax in any amount, large or small, can be levied to support any religious activities or institutions, whatever they may be called. Neither a state nor the Federal Government can, openly or secretly, participate in the affairs of any religious organizations or groups, or vice versa. In the words of Jefferson, the clause against establishment of religion by law was intended to erect "a wall of separation between church and state."[22]

In later cases, Justice Black stressed that "a union of government and religion tends to destroy government and to degrade religion." "Religion is too personal, too sacred, [and] too holy, to permit its 'unhallowed perversion' by a civil magistrate."[23] Religion is also too

---

[21] See ibid. and Philip A. Hamburger, *Separation of Church and State* (Cambridge, MA: Harvard University Press, 2002), 219-229, 321-322, 340-341, 412-418.

[22] *Everson v. Board of Education*, 330 U.S. 1, 15-16.

[23] *Engel v. Vitale*, 370 U.S. 421, 430–432 (1962).

powerful, too sinister, and too greedy to permit its unhindered pervasion of a civil magistracy. "[T]he same powerful religious propagandists" who are allowed to succeed in making one inroad on the state and its laws, Justice Black wrote, "doubtless will continue their propaganda, looking toward complete domination and supremacy of their particular brand of religion. And it is nearly always by insidious approaches that the citadels of [religious] liberty are more successfully attacked."[24] "The First Amendment has erected a wall of separation between church and state. That wall must be kept high and impregnable. We could not approve the slightest breach."[25]

The Supreme Court applied its strict separationist logic with special vigor in cases challenging the traditional state patronage and protection of religious education. In more than two dozen cases after *Everson*, the Court held that public schools could not offer prayers or moments of silence, could not read Scripture or religious texts, could not house Bibles or prayerbooks, could not teach theology or creationism, could not display Decalogues or crèches, could not use the services or facilities of religious bodies. At the same time, states could not provide salary and service supplements to religious schools, could not reimburse them for administering standardized tests, could not lend them state-prescribed textbooks, supplies, films, or counseling services, and could not allow tax deductions or credits for religious school tuition. The Court purged religion from the public school and removed religious schools from many traditional forms of state support.[26]

In *Lemon v. Kurtzman* (1971), the Court distilled the separationist logic of its early cases into a general test to be used in all establishment clause cases. Henceforth every law challenged under the establishment clause would pass constitutional muster only if it could be shown (1) to have a secular purpose; (2) to have a primary effect

---

[24] *Board of Education v. Allen*, 392 U.S. 236, 251–252 (1968) (Black, J., dissenting).
[25] *Everson*, 330 U.S. at 18.
[26] RCE, 191-214.

that neither advances nor inhibits religion; and (3) to foster no excessive entanglement between church and state.[27] When read strictly, the *Lemon* test rendered the establishment clause a formidable obstacle to many traditional forms and forums of church-state cooperation. Particularly the lower courts used this *Lemon* test to outlaw all manner of government subsidies for religious charities, social services, and mission works, government use of religious services, facilities, and publications, and much more. Eventually, it did not take law suits to effectuate these reforms. Particularly local governments, sensitive to the political and fiscal costs of constitutional litigation, often voluntarily ended their prayers, removed their Decalogues, and closed their coffers to religion long before any case was filed against them.

## Separation of Church and State Today

While the *Lemon* test remains formally in place, the strict separation of church and state is no longer the law of the land. In the past two decades, the Supreme Court has abandoned much of its earlier separationism and reversed several of its harshest precedents on this point. In more than a dozen cases, the Court has upheld government policies that support the public access and activities of religious groups—so long as these religious groups are voluntary and so long as non-religious groups are treated the same way. Religious counsellors could be funded as part of a broader federal family counselling program. Religious student groups could have equal access to public classrooms that were open to non-religious student groups. Religious groups could have the same access to public facilities, forums, and funds that were already opened to other civic groups. Religious student newspapers were just as entitled to public university funding as those of non-religious student groups. Religious schools were just as entitled to participate in a state-sponsored school voucher program as other private schools. Religious and non-religious parties that are like-positioned can now usually count on equal treatment and

---

[27] 403 U.S. 602 (1971).

protection from the federal courts, and from many state courts as well.[28]

While religion today usually gets equal treatment from the courts, it sometimes gets special treatment from the American legislature. Over the past 25 years, as the Supreme Court relaxed its application of separation of church and state, Congress began expanding its accommodation of religion by government. In well over two hundred separate pieces of legislation and regulation issued since 1990, Congress has built in new special exemptions, privileges, immunities, benefits, and treatments for religious parties. These are not just the familiar 501(c)(3) income tax exemptions for religious groups or the famous Religious Freedom Restoration Act (RFRA) and its successor, the Religious Land Use and Institutional Persons Act (RLUIPA). Largely unnoticed by the public and largely unchecked by the courts is a vast sprawling network of special religious rights that have been steadily sown into federal laws governing all manner of subjects—laws of evidence and civil procedure, disability, labour, employment, unions, civil rights, interstate commerce, bankruptcy, ERISA, workplace, military, immigration and naturalization, food and drugs, prisons, hospitals, land use, and much more. And federal laws are only part of this network. State laws creating special religious rights for some of these same areas, as well as for local issues like property tax, zoning, non-profit organizations, education, charity, and the like number in the thousands.

These recent cases and statutes, in my view, have ultimately served to enhance religious freedom in America rather than contract it. It must be remembered that separation of church and state is only one principle that the establishment clause embraces, and that the establishment clause is only one guarantee the First Amendment embraces for the protection of religious liberty, the other being the free exercise clause. The First Amendment says: "Congress shall make no law respecting an establishment of religion or prohibiting the free exercise thereof." These two religion clauses, in my view, hold

---

[28] RCE, 184-85, 198-204, 214-20.

complementary guarantees of religious freedom. The free exercise clause outlaws government proscriptions of religion—actions that unduly burden the conscience, restrict religious expression, discriminate against religion, or invade the autonomy of churches and other religious bodies. The establishment clause outlaws government prescriptions of religion—actions that coerce the conscience, mandate forms of religious expression, discriminate in favour of religion, or improperly ally the state with churches or other religious bodies. There can be no burden on, and no coercion of, conscience; no undue restrictions on, and no undue mandating of, religious expression; no discrimination against, and no discrimination for, religion; no government intrusions within, and no government alliances with, religious bodies. Read together this way, the First Amendment free exercise and no-establishment guarantees afford reciprocal and complementary protections to liberty of conscience, freedom of religious exercise, religious equality of a plurality of peaceable faiths, and separation of church and state.

When viewed in isolation, the principle of separation of church and state serves religious liberty best when it is used prudentially, not categorically. Separationism needs to be retained, particularly for its ancient insight of protecting religious bodies from the state and for its more recent insight of protecting the consciences of religious believers from violations by government or religious bodies. Today, as much as in the past, government officials have no constitutional business interfering in the internal affairs of peaceable religious groups. Religious officials have no constitutional business converting the offices of government into instruments of their mission and ministry. Government has no business funding, sponsoring, or actively involving itself in the core religious exercises of a particular religious group or religious official alone. Religious groups have no business drawing on government sponsorship or funding for their core religious exercises. All such conduct violates the basic understanding of separation of church and state and should be outlawed.

The principle of separation of church and state, however, also needs to be contained, and not used as an anti-religious weapon in the culture wars of the public square, the public school, or the public court. Separationism must be viewed as a shield, not a sword in the great struggle to achieve religious freedom for all. A categorical insistence on the principle of separation of church and state in its fifth and strictest sense avails us rather little.

James Madison warned already in 1833 that "it may not be easy, in every possible case, to trace the line of separation between the rights of Religion and the Civil authority, with such distinctness, as to avoid collisions & doubts on unessential points."[29] This caveat has become even more salient today. The modern welfare state, for better or worse, reaches deeply into virtually all aspects of modern life—through its network of education, charity, welfare, child care, health care, construction, zoning, workplace, taxation, and sundry other regulations. Madison's solution was "an entire abstinence of the Government from interference [with religion] in any way whatever, beyond the necessity of preserving public order, & protecting each sect against trespasses on its legal rights by others."[30] This traditional understanding of a minimal state role in the life of society in general, and of religious bodies in particular—however alluring it may be in theory—is no longer realistic in practice.

It is thus even more imperative today than in Madison's day that the principle of separation of church and state not be pressed to reach what Madison called the "unessentials." It is one thing for the Court to outlaw daily Christian prayers and broadcasted Bible readings from the public school, quite another thing to ban moments of silence and private displays of the Decalogue in the same schools. It is one thing to bar direct tax support for religious education, quite another thing to bar tax deductions for parents who wish to educate their children in the faith. It is one thing to prevent government officials from

---

[29] Letter to Rev. Jaspar Adams (1833), in Daniel L. Dreisbach, *Religion and Politics in the Early Republic: Jasper Adams and the Church-State Debate* (Lexington, KY: University Press of Kentucky, 1996), 117-121, at 120 (emphasis added).

[30] Quoted by ibid., 120.

delegating their core police powers to religious bodies, quite another thing to prevent them from facilitating the charitable services of voluntary religious and non-religious associations alike. It is one thing to outlaw governmental prescriptions of prayers, ceremonies, and symbols in public forums, quite another thing to outlaw governmental accommodations of private prayers, ceremonies, and symbols in public forums. To press separationist logic too deeply into "unessentials" not only "trivializes" the place of religion in public and private life, as Stephen Carter argues.[31] It also trivializes the power of the constitution, converting it from a code of cardinal principles of national law into a codex of petty precepts of local life.

Too zealous an interpretation of the principle of separation of church and state also runs afoul of other constitutive principles of the First Amendment—particularly the principles of liberty of conscience and religious equality. The Court must be at least as zealous in protecting religious conscience from secular coercion as protecting secular conscience from religious coercion. The Court should be at least as concerned to ensure the equal treatment of religion as to ensure the equality of religion and non-religion. It is no violation of the principle of separation of church and state when a legislature or court accommodates judiciously the conscientious scruples of a religious individual or the cardinal callings of a religious body. It is also no violation of this principle when government grants religious individuals and institutions equal access to state benefits, public forums, or tax disbursements that are open to non-religionists similarly situated. To do otherwise is, indeed, to move toward what Justice Stewart once called "the establishment of a religion of secularism."[32]

---

[31] Stephen L. Carter, *The Culture of Disbelief: How American Law and Politics Trivializes Religious Devotion* (New York: Basic Books, 1993).

[32] *Abington School District v. Schempp*, 374 U.S. 203, 313 (Stewart, J., dissenting).

# 6

## THE AMERICAN FOUNDERS AND THE PROBLEM OF CIVIL RELIGION: TRUTH AND UTILITY

*Scott Yenor*

The greatest 19th century observers of the American scene seemed to think that the future of America's experiment in self-government depended on cultivating the correct moral foundation, which in turn depended, in part, at least, on American civil religion. The qualities of character that these thinkers considered necessary for the American Experiment to be successful were byproducts of healthy modern religious belief. Alexis de Tocqueville praised Christianity for reinforcing orderly family life, for fostering the personal self-control essential to self-government, for grounding Americans' penchant for joining civil associations, for confining the otherwise audacious plans of modern Americans, and for reconciling Americans, at times, to the imperfection of their condition. One might add that Christianity's *imago deo* supports the idea of equal and inalienable individual rights as a source of democratic justice. Tocqueville's praise of American civil religion is all the more remarkable, I would submit, because Tocqueville thought Christianity was a leading part in the "tyranny of the majority" in America, where Christianity mingled with public opinion to draw "a formidable circle around thought" in a way that was nevertheless "doubtless good."[1]

Tocqueville provides a classic exposition of what civil religion means in thus defending civil religion in America: "If it serves man very much as an individual that his religion be true, this is not so for

---

[1] Tocqueville, *Democracy in America*, Translated by Harvey C. Mansfield, Jr. and Delba Winthrop (University of Chicago Press, 2000), 244, 245 (1.2.7). For the benefits that Christianity brings democracy in America, see 1.2.9, pp. 278ff.

society. Society has nothing to fear or to hope from the other life; and what is most important to it is not so much that all citizens profess the true religion, but that they profess a religion."[2] Tocqueville drills deeper than the American Founders ever did in all of these respects, but generally the American Founders, at their best, embrace a similar view of religion as crucial to shaping the public opinion for a self-governing people. Such statements could be multiplied, of course, but allow only a few of the most famous to suffice. Perhaps the most famous is in George Washington's Farewell Address:

> Of all the disposition and habits which lead to political prosperity, Religion and Morality are indispensable supports. In vain would that man claim the tribute of Patriotism, who should labour to subvert these great Pillars of human happiness, these firmest props of the duties of men and citizens. The mere politician, equally with the pious man ought to cherish and respect them. A volume could not trace all their connections with private and public felicity. Let it simply be asked where is there security for property, for reputation, for life, if the sense of religious obligation desert the oaths, which are the instruments of investigation in Courts of Justice? And let us with caution indulge the supposition, that morality can be maintained without religion. Whatever may be conceded to the influence of refined education on minds of peculiar structure, reason and experience forbid us to expect that National morality can prevail in exclusion of religious belief.[3]

---

[2] Tocqueville, *Democracy in America*, 278 (1.2.9).

[3] Washington, "Farewell Address" in *George Washington: A Collection*, Edited by W.B. Allen (Liberty Fund, 1988), 521. Consider as well Article 3 of the Northwest Ordinance:

> Religion, morality, and knowledge, being necessary to good government and the happiness of mankind, schools and the means of education shall forever be encouraged. The utmost good faith shall always be observed towards the Indians; their lands and property shall never be taken from them without their consent; and, in their property, rights, and liberty, they shall never be invaded or disturbed, unless in just and lawful wars authorized by Congress; but laws

Rarely advocating the employment of public power to promote religion directly, Washington seeks support for what Tocqueville would call the indirect influence of religion on morality. The statesmanlike response is to "cherish and respect" religion and morality for positive effects on "National morality." Thus we have the Founders supporting religion as a basis for family life and education and respect for the rights of man and so on—much in the spirit of Tocqueville.

For my purposes, I am going to assume that Tocqueville and the American Founders are broadly of like minds on the question of civic religion. This is as important for what Tocqueville and the Founders are *not* as much as for what they are. Neither Tocqueville nor the Founders embrace anything like a Roman or a neo-Roman or a Rousseauian conception of civil religion. Under this conception, the gods are the gods of the city and all of the political community's principles are divine and civic: such a civic religion binds and constitutes the political community, giving it identity, purpose and direction. Such "strong civil religions" (as I call them) bind patriotism and otherworldly beliefs and supply a commanding set of truths that make the pursuit of common purposes more likely amid a world of otherwise disparate human beings. In times of crisis such commanding truths make common action possible. Such civic piety rules the public square too directly and tends (from a Christian point of view) in the direction of idolatry of the state. Neither do Tocqueville and the Founders embrace a "naked public square." Each defends the important public value of religious belief in a limited government or a government that distinguishes public from private goods, because each recognizes that private beliefs and practices have profound public import.

So the American Founders and Tocqueville are broadly on the same team in embracing a "weak" civil religion that accepts the

---

founded in justice and humanity, shall from time to time be made for preventing wrongs being done to them, and for preserving peace and friendship with them.

indirect influence of Christianity on public opinion in a country where public opinion rules.[4] Theirs is an in between position: between a too civic civil religion and an insufficiently religious public opinion or public square; or between a civic religion that melds church and state and one that separates church and state such that never the twain shall meet.

There is much truth to this point of view. Yet in thinking through the "utility" of civil religion for each group of thinkers, we come to see that their visions for the utility of civil religion are actually quite different—they point very much to a different understanding of the origin of religion in the human soul and a different understanding of what constitutes a society. Tocqueville's religious psychology seems much more open to religion being true than the American Founders' account of these matters. This means that, in the long term, also much more open to religion, accidentally perhaps, being both useful and a permanent feature of the human condition. The American Founders present what can only called a typically enlightened view of religion and its place in the social order, while Tocqueville's view reflects a serious critique of this enlightened view.

Let us first consider the American Founders. What I am going to argue here may sound radically reductive, and nothing could be further from my intent. The American Founders were broadly of one mind on religion and its relation to the political order. There were serious disagreements among the Founders over secondary matters—and these are the matters that divide the American populace even today. In light of history, what is most remarkable about the American Founding is that there was no dispute over whether there

---

[4] Thus the almost ritual invocation of both Tocqueville and the American Founders among thinkers who recognize the importance of civil religion to early American political practice, see, for instance, Michael Zuckert, "John Locke and the Problem of Civil Religion" and Walter Berns, "Religion and the Founding Principle" in *The Moral Foundations of the American Republic*, Edited by Robert Horowitz (Virginia University Press, 1986).

should be freedom of conscience or the free exercise of religion, there was no dispute about what the origin of government derived from the consent of the governed (as opposed to from God), and there was no attempt in the un-amended Constitution to secure a special place for public worship or for cultivating Christian duties. Religious freedom depends on a non-religious source. The Declaration of Independence, however much it may ultimately owe to Christianity, is a conscious part of the Founders' enlightened movement to dethrone, destroy, or displace the authority of revealed religion in politics. Much of the hard work of subordinating revealed religion to politics was done, in America, so the Founders rarely had to conduct (and hence rarely conducted) European-style frontal assaults on revealed religion; their advances were but mop up advances of those Founders (notably Jefferson and Madison) who were most interested in diminishing the political authority of revealed Christianity.

The Founders were divided on secondary matters—whether, to borrow from one scholar, government "depended in some way on religion and, therefore, whether it should be permitted, in some way, to foster religion, and whether this should be done at the federal as well as the state level."[5] Some state constitutions prevented discrimination among religious sects, but seemed to allow distinctions between believers and non-believers. There was also legitimate disagreement over whether or under what circumstances religious belief and practice would be useful in the *novus ordo seclorum*. There were debates about how best to support a useful Christianity masking a somewhat deeper debate over how useful Christianity ultimately was. It is no surprise that these are the questions that continue to dog us today—they are the ground of dispute in our constitutional order from the beginning. While our institutions and the foundation of our governments do not presuppose a Supreme Being, their preservation seems to presuppose one.[6]

---

[5] Berns, "Religion and the Founding Principle," 210. Much of the preceding paragraph is traceable to Berns' observations as well.

[6] Berns, "Religion and the Founding Principle," 212.

The Massachusetts Constitution, among the last of those written in post-Revolutionary America, is perhaps the high water mark of the American Founding's pro-religion constitutions. Not only does that document declare it to be the right and duty of "towns, parishes, precincts, and other bodies politic to provide monies for the support of the public worship of God," but it also, significantly, suggests that each man should so worship "according to the dictates of his own conscience" and that this was to be done so as to promote "the happiness of a people and the good order and preservation of civil government" which "essentially depend upon piety, religion, and morality."[7] The Massachusetts Constitution, in other words, considers religion from a political point of view, just as Washington had in his Farewell Address—always mindful of the rights of conscience and that government supports religion for the sake of social and political health. Those aspects of religious belief consistent with natural rights philosophy were admitted into the public order and they were embraced insofar as they helped to establish a liberal society.[8] What is acutely missing among the Founders, however, is a long, penetrating, detailed account of why religious belief is useful: it is a position more often asserted than explained or elaborated upon. Their argument involves some dot connecting, which I have tried to conduct elsewhere. It involves efforts to teach the morality of family life and encourage responsible exercises of freedom.[9]

The overall agreement among the American Founders on first principles involved the religious subordination to politics—and

---

[7] Massachusetts Constitution, Article III.

[8] The Massachusetts Constitution, Washington's Farewell Address, and Jefferson's Query 19 on Manners ("And Can the liberties of a nation be thought secure when we have removed their only firm basis, a conviction in the minds of the people that these liberties are of the gift of God?) all speak with one voice on this matter.

[9] See Scott Yenor, "The True Origin of Society: The Founders and the Family" in First Principles Series (Heritage Foundation, 2014): http://www.heritage.org/research/reports/2013/10/the-true-origin-of-society-the-founders-on-the-family

religion's usefulness depends on the needs of politics. Disagreements intruded at precisely this point. Washington and others worried that a political community founded on the rights of man could not long endure without the outside intervention of religious belief, while other thinkers (notably Madison, it seems) were less inclined to worry about the persistence of religious belief as a prop for free government. Efforts to divine the Founders' intentions on issues surrounding the utility and strategies surrounding religious belief are, no doubt, often shaped by one's own views on how useful religious belief is or over what strategies can best lead to a more effective religious belief.

To Tocqueville's eyes, the Founders' perspective on the utility of religious belief had penetrated into the popular mind. "I do not know if all Americans have faith in their religion," writes Tocqueville, "for who can read to the bottom of hearts?—but I am sure that they believe it necessary to the maintenance of republican institutions. This opinion does not belong only to one class of citizens or to one party, but to the entire nation; one finds it in all ranks."[10] In America, "the sovereign is religious, and consequently hypocrisy ought to be common."[11] How common? Contrast the hypocrisy in Roman civil religion as seen in Augustine's Varro and in the Americans of Tocqueville's telling.[12] Varro distinguished between civil and natural theology—the former, established by laws in pagan cities, was a false collection of frivolous fantasies suited to the vulgar capacities of those who could believe but not know, while the latter was the domain of philosophic knowers and patricians who knew the importance of the obedience extracted by the civic religion. Knowers and patricians could mock religion behind closed doors but prudence demanded from them an outward adherence to religious rites and forms for the sake of the obedience civic religion supplies. Hypocrisy is limited to

---

[10] Tocqueville, *Democracy in America*, 280 (1.2.9).
[11] Tocqueville, *Democracy in America*, 278 (1.2.9).
[12] See Pierre Manent, *Tocqueville and the Nature of Democracy*, pp. 91ff.

the ruling class.[13] American hypocrisy is democratized to an extent, and the obedience to religion is still extracted from all or most. Like the patricians of Rome, many Americans keep up appearances with uncertain faith; like the plebeians, those Americans nevertheless obey in order to ensure the well-functioning of democratic society.

Tocqueville has a deeper understanding of the threats to a well-functioning liberal democracy and he has a deeper and, I presume to say, more religious understanding of religion's utility in a democracy. American religion was not simply or most importantly a regulator of morality or, in the fashion of the Romans, an inducer of obedience to the city's laws or to the sacrifices that people make in times of trouble. Religion did regulate mores through women, Tocqueville suggests, but it was not the only factor in regulating the family (America's respect for nature also explains this). Tocqueville is quite clear that respect for the law and the sacrifices Americans are willing to make to public spirited endeavors are NOT traceable to religious belief, but are traceable to the American conviction of self-interest rightly understood and self-government. Americans respect law because it is their own; they defend the country as their own.[14] The civil religion is useful in an entirely different way from how it was useful under the old order.

A new understanding of the utility of religion is needed for a world itself new, to paraphrase Tocqueville himself. Religion, for Tocqueville, keeps Americans from doing and daring everything.

> Revolutionaries in America are obliged to profess openly a certain respect for the morality and equity of Christianity, which does not permit them to violate its laws easily when they are opposed to the execution of their designs....Up to now, no one has been encountered

---

[13] St. Augustine, *City of God*, Translated by Marcus Dods (Modern Library, 1993), VI, 4-7 (pp. 188-196). Perhaps this is the point of view that Washington defends in his Farewell Address.

[14] Consider, for instance, Tocqueville, *Democracy in America*, 1.2.6: "On Public Spirit in the United States" (pp. 225ff), "On the Idea of Rights in the United States" (pp. 227ff), and "On Respect for the Law in the United States" (pp. 229ff).

in the United States who dared to advance the maxim that everything is permitted in the interest of society. An impious maxim—one that seems to have been invented in a century of freedom to legitimate all the tyrants to come.[15]

What Christianity teaches are the limits of human power, the limits of our ability to control the world—this essentially conservative or somewhat quiescent disposition, part of the Christian faith, is strong precisely where democracy tends to be tempted and dangerous. Modern peoples, and especially Americans, are tempted to adopt a dangerous interpretation of the dogma of the sovereignty of the people—an assertion of power to remake the world entirely, to assert a human sovereignty over all of our world, to make the world perfect, I am tempted to say. It is in combating this tendency that Tocqueville sees the greatest contributions of American Christianity. The power of natural religion or the natural power of religion rests on its natural disgust for existence and the immense desire to exist and the hope that this situation will be remedied in eternity. Christian teaching makes use of these natural tendencies and thus, as a "natural-revealed" religion, is situated to govern democracy's dangerous tendencies.

This position on the political utility of religion involves difficulty, as Tocqueville acknowledges. America still is, Tocqueville writes, "the place in the world where the Christian religion has preserved genuine powers over souls."[16] Religion would seem to have genuine force in human souls when it is sincerely believed—believed for its content and the way it shapes one's view of the world. America has tended to leave religion in its "natural state," resting on man's "natural disgust for existence" and his "immense desire to exist." Religion is "only a particular form of hope, and it is as natural to the human heart as hope itself."[17] When embraced for its utility as opposed to its truth, it rests neither on hope nor on these psychological dispositions; useful religion is *unnatural* and hence

---

[15] Tocqueville, *Democracy in America*, 280 (1.2.9).
[16] Tocqueville, *Democracy in America*, 278 (1.2.9).
[17] Tocqueville, *Democracy in America*, 284 (1.2.9).

unstable in how it sits in the human soul. Such utility democratized cannot but weaken and corrupt religion. Pierre Manent, calling this the "central difficulty of the Tocquevillian interpretation of the relation of democracy and religion," puts this thought with the greatest clarity: "The religion of the Americans loses its utility proportional to their attachment to it for reasons of utility."[18]

The importance of this problem can be seen through a comparison of the Founders' views on the "non-religious" position with Tocqueville's "non-religious" position. The Founders barely imagined a situation where a whole body of the people did not believe: they still fixed their eyes on some of the debris that defined the old world as they articulated principles to guide the new world; they worried about excessive religious zeal. For Tocqueville, religious indifference and "negative doctrines" were the primary threats to democracy. "Carried along by an insensible current against which they do not have the courage to struggle and to which they nonetheless yield with regret, they abandon the faith that they love to follow the doubt that leads them to despair."[19] Such unbelievers can still judge religion useful and respect and encourage religious practice so that there is a predominantly religious public opinion, but that solution cannot work in the long term if more and more people take the patrician attitude.

So Tocqueville leaves us with a terrific tension. Christianity holds that the world is imperfect and fallen, while modern democracy flatters our capacity to perfect the world with our own powers. Christianity limits the vision of democracy so long as it is believed or so long as its tendency to limit the ambitions of democracy is widely shared among the populace. It will be an enemy of democracy once democratic ambitions exceed Christian bounds or Christianity will adapt itself to democratic demands.[20] There is a tendency in the

---

[18] Manent, *Tocqueville and the Nature of Democracy*, 91.

[19] Tocqueville, *Democracy in America*, 287 (1.2.9).

[20] This is the situation in Tocqueville's France and possibly in our contemporary America, where there are those who know only doubt or

human mind to "*harmonize* the earth with heaven,"[21] which puts them on a collision course. If the Christian disposition erodes in the mind, it is hard to see how it can govern democracy. Once modern people provide a modern account for the religious psychology, doctrinal indifference cannot resist the movements of the democratic heart.

Where does this leave us? Religious utility depends on religious truth, and believers in the modern world should seek to defend the truth of religion in precisely the location where religion lays on top of human psychology. Religion contributes to morality, but that is not where it thinks of its own truth; morality is a byproduct, not its essence. Defend the essence of religious belief—that is where it can appeal to human nature and that is where it is most useful in a democracy. It has the additional benefit of being true.

---

indifference to religion and publicly abjure the faith of their fathers (or the implications of the faith of their fathers) and this provokes a reaction from those still devoted to the faith. In France, this battle ended up leading to a battle over control of the state and over the acceptability of democracy as such, while in our America it is a battle over the acceptable range of public opinion but it points to a battle over the acceptability of modern ideas and institutions as such.

[21] Tocqueville, *Democracy in America*, 275 (1.2.9).

# 7

## THE FOUNDERS, HOBBY LOBBY, AND THE HHS MANDATE

### David Ramsey

In the aftermath of the Supreme Court's recent ruling in *Burwell v. Hobby Lobby*[1]—which had the dubious honor of being acknowledged in the *Harvard Law Review* as a blockbuster case months before the Court handed down its ruling[2]—it might seem that religious liberty is headed for a period of rebirth and renewal in American politics. But those who turn to the Court's ruling in the case in search of a coherent defense of religious liberty will likely come away disappointed. Far from finding in Justice Alito's majority opinion a spirited defense of the First Amendment's instruction that Congress shall make no law prohibiting the free exercise of religion, we discover, rather, a tangle of qualifications and provisos leading up to an incredibly narrow holding. The only matter decided by the Court was to grant the closely held for-profit corporations in question exemptions, pursuant to the provisions of the amended Religious Freedom and Restoration Act, from the mandate of the Department of Health and Human Services that all businesses with more than 50 employees opting to provide health care to those employees must include in their health care plans access to all Food and Drug Administration-approved contraceptive methods. Plaintiffs sought to

---

[1] *Burwell, Secretary of Health and Human Services, et al. v. Hobby Lobby Stores, Inc., et al.* 573 U.S. \_\_\_\_ (2014)

[2] Alan J. Meese and Nathan B. Oman, *"Hobby Lobby,* Corporate Law, and the Theory of the Firm: Why for-profit corporations are RFRA persons," 127 *Harvard Law Review* 273 (2014).

exclude from their coverage only those means of contraception—plan B, RU-486 and two intrauterine devices—which act as abortifacients, preventing implantation of a fertilized egg in the uterus. In support of their exclusion of such drugs and devices, plaintiffs explained that their religion teaches that to be involved in the termination of human life after conception is a sin.[3] While the plaintiffs, when explaining their objections to the HHS mandate, speak in terms of their religion, both the Court and counsel for the government agencies employ a highly specialized, technical language derived from centuries of case law and decades of administrative policymaking. The particulars of the case and the intervening precedent threaten to cloud the clear waters of our constitutional theory. When Chief Justice Marshall wrote in *McCulloch v. Maryland* that "we must never forget that it is a *constitution* we are expounding," it was in the context of distinguishing the easily accessible, general terms of the Constitution from the highly specialized language required to produce a legal code.[4] It was one of Marshall's greatest achievements as Chief Justice to make of the prolixity of the legal codes with which he was confronted such cogent, well-organized and readable legal arguments. In the following pages I will first review the elements of the law upon which the Court's *Hobby Lobby* ruling is built, then assess the Court's opinion, and the two principal separate opinions, from the vantage of the American constitutional tradition, and finally conclude with some reflections on what this case can tell us about the Court's devotion to protecting religious liberty today. Students of the great books have

---

[3] Cf. Brief for HHS in No. 13-354, pp. 9-10, n.4 and 573 U.S. \_\_\_\_\_ (2014) J. Alito, 12.

[4] "A Constitution, to contain an accurate detail of all the subdivisions of which its great powers will admit, and of all the means by which they may be carried into execution, would partake of the prolixity of a legal code, and could scarcely be embraced by the human mind. It would probably never be understood by the public. Its nature, therefore, requires that only its great outlines should be marked, its important objects designated, and the minor ingredients which compose those objects be deduced from the nature of the objects themselves." 17 U.S. 316 (1819) at 407.

good reason to pause periodically and assess the status of protections for religious liberty, as we do in the pages which follow, as it seems likely that the serious study of the great books can only flourish in those societies which remain devoted to the enlightened and tolerant principle of liberty of conscience enshrined in the First Amendment.

## Constitutional Theory

One of the hallmarks of American constitutionalism is its focus on maintaining meaningful distinctions or 'separation' between the powers of government, and it is certainly one of the principal roles of the Supreme Court to maintain those powers as distinct and separate over time. According to the theory of the founders, it is we the people who, through the medium of the Constitution, have delegated some of our power in order to better secure the limited goods or ends enumerated in the Preamble. By making adequate provision for a strong national government, we hope to preserve those rights or liberties not delegated to the government. One sign of this adequate provision in the Constitution is that the power we have delegated is immediately partitioned (as evinced by the vesting clauses with which each of the first three articles of the Constitution begin) into separate powers: legislative, executive, judicial. These powers are to be housed in distinct institutions—a bicameral legislature, a unitary executive, an independent judiciary—composed of differing numbers of individuals. In Congress we find the many, but divided against itself into the tumultuous and ever-changing multitude of the House, whose entire body may be displaced periodically through the mechanism of biannual national elections, and the more statesmanlike and equitable Senate, whose number is fixed—or rather remains fixed in a stable proportion to the number of states in the union—whose form is granted more stability through the mechanism of protecting two thirds of its membership from political pressure during each biannual election, and whose six-year terms in office allow them to outlast both Representatives and the President. It is the function of the Congress to make law. Ours was to be a republic, a regime in which laws, and not men, would rule. In order to ensure that the process of lawmaking is not undertaken rashly, the founders saw fit to provide a widespread and diverse representation of the opinions present within the regime, and to constitute the body charged with making law in such a way as to ensure adequate deliberation. Let this suffice for our consideration of the legislative power in itself.

In at least one respect, the founders seem to have agreed with Montesquieu, who held that the beginning of tyranny, and the source of all deprivation of individual liberty, is to be found in the union of the legislative and the executive powers in one person or group of persons.[5] In order to preserve individual liberty, then, the legislative and executive functions must be channeled into distinct entities, housed in separate institutions. But unlike the legislative function, the executive functions—enforcing the laws, securing the nation from domestic unrest and external threats—are best carried out when applied by a unitary actor, possessed with all the necessary characteristics of action, among which we might enumerate decision, activity, secrecy and dispatch.[6] Though the President is to be provided with ample access to counsel in the separate departments to be established by Congress, it is worth noting that the President of Article II in the Constitution consults with no named department heads when making his decisions about how best to carry out the laws provided by Congress. These departments were to be supplied by Congress at a later date, and are subject to periodic revision. If Congress was designed in such a way as to give voice to the Many when exercising its legislative power, the President possesses the unique vantage and characteristics of the One, and never more so than when he takes action.

---

[5] Montesquieu, *The Spirit of the Laws,* trans. and ed. Anne M. Cohler, Basia C. Miller and Harold S. Stone (New York: Cambridge University Press, 1989), Bk XI, Ch 6, 157.

[6] Alexander Hamilton, James Madison and John Jay. *The Federalist* with Letters of "Brutus," ed. Terence Ball (New York: Cambridge University Press, 2003), *Federalist 70,* 342.

When turning to consider the *time* for and within which the executive acts, it is most characteristically that of the moment, the "now." By way of contrast, the legislative power comes to light as a mean between the ever-present executive and the judiciary, whose view—especially as we rise to the vantage of the Supreme Court—must reach beyond the immediate and the interim terms, stretching back to the debates of the Philadelphia Convention and the common law heritage which preceded it, and forward to the consideration of future lines of growth within the law. The Court must, to a certain extent, consider the future when taking action, but the nature of the appellate proceeding draws its gaze most often to the past—reviewing the factual record and the disposition of the present case as it moved through the lower courts, the debates which took place while Congress was giving shape to the law at hand, and the fittingness of that law when placed within the network of statutes which has been built upon our fundamental law, the Constitution. The law of Congress appears more clearly as "mere" policy when contrasted with the constitutional law that must remain the concern of the courts, and Justices on the Court are led, upon consideration of the Court's institutional strengths and weaknesses, to exercise restraint when called upon to enact without legislative support those policies which they might prefer to see enacted, or to nullify those policies of which they disapprove.

We expect our Presidents to confidently lead the nation in crisis, and to give force to the laws provided by Congress. We understand that those laws must most often be a product of compromise, resisting the partisan impulse to institute a final solution to the problem at hand, and we look to Congress to broker such compromises. In both instances, the Constitution entrusts the people with the responsibility of assessing the activities of the political branches through periodic elections, in part because the nature of the work is relatively easy to assess. But the great victories of the Court are rarely appreciated in the short or intermediate term. The measure of judicial power must always remain the strength of its precedent, its ability to ensure that the fabric of law remains fitted to the fundamental design of the

Constitution. The founders deemed that such work was best left neither to the One nor the Many but rather to the Few, who were to be insulated from the great majority of political pressures by guaranteeing to them fixed salaries and uninterrupted service during good behavior.

But we would be remiss to view the separation of powers as solely a precautionary measure. We must also consider the argument from the standpoint of the founders' concern for ensuring institutional efficacy. The founders understood that the distinct functions of the government are best carried out by different groupings of individuals. Among the coordinate branches of government established by the Constitution, Congress alone is divided into parts. While this certainly helps to check the ever-present danger of faction in a republican regime,[7] it also ensures robust debate during the drafting phase of the legislative process, making it more unlikely that Congress will be able to pass on many bills to the President until they have received due consideration. While the characteristics of executive action requiring a unified executive were treated above, it may also prove instructive to consider the possibilities for intrigue and the difficulties with Presidential accountability which would arise if the Constitution had instituted a plural executive. In order to ensure adequate rigor in the selection of judges to be granted fixed salaries and service during good behavior, the founders incorporated the assessments of both political branches. But in so doing it is important to recall that under the Constitution of 1787, neither Senators[8] nor the President were subject to direct election. In the case of the former, the voice of the people was filtered through the state legislature, in that of the latter, through the electoral college. Moreover, we note the implied balance between state and national government in the process of judicial selection—while the national

---

[7] *Federalist 10.*

[8] The 17th Amendment changed the method and mode of electing U.S. Senators.

representative has the initiative, his power can be checked by the states.

This leads to our final reflection on the constitutional theory relevant to the case at hand. The founders did not understand themselves to be at liberty to create society anew. The nature of their making was to take up the materials that were readily available in the society around them, and form them into a more perfect union. If there were time, we might stop to review the many similarities between the Articles of Confederation and the Constitution. Though there were important departures from that model, the national government established by the Constitution is colored by the component parts and semi-sovereign wholes out of which it is composed, the states. Even the language of the Constitution is conservative, importing legal concepts developed over centuries within the English common law tradition.[9] Finally, we note that just as the Constitution did not attempt to make a complete break with the past, neither did it preclude the possibility of change in the future. Rather, it made allowances for such changes. In the following section we turn to the applications of Article V, and to a handful of those constitutional amendments, both formal and informal.

## Constitutional Policy: Free Exercise and Patents, Corporations and Regulatory Agencies

Having first taken our bearings from the institutional arrangements set out in the Constitution, we now turn to the three constitutional innovations in conflict in the *Hobby Lobby* case: religious liberty, corporate personhood, and the "quasi-legislative, quasi-judicial" role of administrative and regulatory agencies. About the first, little needs to be said here. There is a rich literature on the debates surrounding

---

[9] James R. Stoner, Jr. *Common Law Liberty: Rethinking American Constitutionalism* (Lawrence, KS: University Press of Kansas, 2003), 1–29.

ratification of the Constitution.[10] To the extent that the Anti-Federalists helped to shape our Constitution through their resistance to quick and easy ratification, their principal achievement may very well have been[11] their insistence that, upon ratification, the Constitution be amended, and a Bill of Rights added to it in the manner characteristic of our English constitutional heritage. For all of their caution in not proposing too radical a break from the political tradition, the Anti-Federalist resistance to the Federalist regime reminds us that the Constitution *did* introduce a number of innovations. It is to the credit of James Madison—who seems not to have believed that a Bill of Rights was necessary given the limited powers delegated to the soundly constructed institutions of the Constitution—that he made passage of a Bill of Rights a priority of the First Congress, bringing order and balance to the diverse proposals for amendments from the state ratifying conventions, and ensuring their rapid progress through the House of Representatives.[12] Madison knew that it would be essential to establish a base of support and veneration for the young Constitution that was as broad as possible.[13] His proposed amendments did a great deal to appease Anti-Federalist fears of consolidated government without

---

[10] Prominent treatments include Douglas Adair, *Fame and the Founding Fathers,* ed. Trevor Colbourn (Indianapolis: Liberty Fund, 1998); Irving Brant, *The Bill of Rights: Its Origins and Meaning* (Indianapolis: Bobbs-Merrill, 1965); David F. Epstein, *The Political Theory of the Federalist* (Chicago: University of Chicago Press, 1984); Jackson Turner Main, *The Antifederalists: Critics of the Constitution 1781-1788* (New York: W.W. Norton & Co., 1974); Michael Allen Gillespie and Michael Lienesch, eds. *Ratifying the Constitution* (Lawrence, KS: University Press of Kansas, 1989); Akhil Reed Amar, *The Bill of Rights: Creation and Reconstruction* (New Haven: Yale University Press, 1997); Pauline Maier, *Ratification: The People Debate the Constitution, 1787-1788* (New York: Simon & Schuster, 2010) and Herbert J. Storing, *What the Anti-Federalists Were* For (Chicago: University of Chicago Press, 1981).

[11] Cf. Storing, *What the Anti-Federalists Were* For, 64 and 71-76.

[12] 1 *Annals of Congress* 431-442 (1789-90).

[13] *Federalist 49.*

compromising the structural integrity, so to speak, of the Constitution itself. Today the provisions of the Bill of Rights, and especially those of the First Amendment, are the constitutional texts most familiar to the American public, and the Court has done a great deal to promote this primacy of place over the last century. As we shall see below, it is certainly one important component of the work of the Court to ensure that the contemporary advocates for the Federalist and Anti-Federalist approaches to American constitutionalism continue to receive adequate consideration.

The remaining constitutional innovations seem to share a common point of origin in Article I, §8, cl. 8, which vests in Congress the power to make laws which will "promote the Progress of Science and of useful Arts, by securing for limited Times to Authors and Inventors the exclusive Right to their respective Writings and Discoveries." The Constitution grants special privileges to those who produce new and useful applications of scientific knowledge. By promising the great boon of allowing inventors to recoup monopoly profits, even for a limited time, from the sale of their novel and useful inventions, protected by copyright and patent, the Constitution incentivized, and thereby ensured the orientation of the great majority of our citizens toward, hopes for progress through the development of applied scientific understanding. Federal protection of intellectual property is a powerful incentive, especially in a society of middle class individuals largely defined by the sturdy if not elevated passions which tend to predominate in a democracy: the fear of violent death and the desire for commodious living. This inconspicuous constitutional provision, which passed through the Philadelphia Convention and the ratification process with very little debate, today serves as something like the keystone supporting America's continued leadership in the development of applied scientific knowledge or technology.

But just as the positive political philosophy of the Federalists called forth the negative critique of constitutionalism which we find in the writings of the Anti-Federalists, so also the Constitution's optimism about the societal progress which an ever-advancing scientific understanding would promote provoked the strongest critique to be leveled against the American regime in the 20th century. The thesis, so to speak, of this critique was that America was nothing more than technology, the ontological embodiment of the disposition toward useful deployment of scientific understanding.[14] While this critique requires an adequate response, it is beyond the scope of this essay to put one forward. But to begin making the case that America is more than devotion to fulfilling the appetites of the average man through scientific understanding applied to the conquest of nature, the reduction of all being to the status of standing reserve, we might seek to build on the attempts of select jurists, beginning with Louis Brandeis, to discover within the constitutional text an unwritten or implied right to privacy.[15] Alternately, we might turn to the specific guarantees of the Bill of Rights, beginning with the First Amendment freedoms of religious exercise, speech, press and association. Taken together, these constitutional resources might become, in the hands of a capable jurist, an adequate basis from which to build a jurisprudence capable of taming or reorienting the impulses inflamed by I.8.8. Indeed, it could very well be the case that the Anti-Federalists' reluctance to ratify the Constitution absent a Bill of Rights was grounded at some level in their mistrust of a charter of government which incentivized the pursuit of scientific understanding without also protecting what Madison would later refer to publicly as the "sacred rights of conscience." [16] If this is the case, then a key to beginning the response called forth by the question concerning technology would seem to rest in a thorough

---

[14] Martin Heidegger, *Introduction to Metaphysics,* trans. Gregory Fried and Richard Polt (New Haven: Yale University Press, 2000), 37-51, esp. 40 and, more generally *The Question Concerning Technology,* trans. William Lovitt (New York: Garland Publishing, 1977).

[15] *Olmstead v U.S.* 277 U.S. 438 (1928), 472-485 (J. Brandeis, dissenting). See also Louis Brandeis and Samuel Warren, "The Right to Privacy," 4 *Harvard Law Review* 193 (1890).

[16] James Madison, "A Proclamation," 23 July 1813 in 2 *A Compilation of the Messages and Papers of the Presidents* 517-518 (New York: Bureau of National Literature, 1897).

consideration of the Anti-Federalist argument. In order to develop a more complete consideration of the problem of technology in America we turn to the Court's development of corporate theory[17] and its gradual accommodation of the legislative policy or orientation adopted by Congress to address these changes in the economic life of the nation: the administrative agency.

The corporation was introduced as a legal form centuries before both the industrial revolution and the American founding. Indeed, the corporate form had been employed by the English Crown for more than a century before Europeans discovered the New World. The first British colonies on the continent, Virginia and Massachusetts Bay, were both joint stock corporations.[18] The corporation has an impressive pedigree. Without recourse to that form, which allowed investors to associate and pool their capital for the sake of a joint venture, it is unlikely that such ambitious projects would have taken shape, and without it they would almost certainly not have done so in such great variety. In his important chapter "On the Point of Departure and Its Importance for the Future of the Anglo-Americans," we recall that Alexis de Tocqueville draws a sharp distinction between the sojourning colonists of Massachusetts Bay, and the "gold-seekers" sent to establish the colony in Virginia.[19] It was the colonists of Massachusetts Bay who understood themselves as called to establish a "city upon a hill," which was to be a model of Christian charity for the world, an answer to the question of why God allows for the divisions between rich and poor, powerful and

---

[17] Morton J. Horwitz, *The Transformation of American Law, 1870-1960: The Crisis of Legal Orthodoxy* (New York: Oxford University Press, 1992), 65-107.

[18] My account of the English and Colonial American experiments with the corporate draws heavily from Alfred H. Kelly, Winfred A. Harbison and Herman Belz, *The American Constitution: Its Origins and Development, Vol. I,* 7th ed (New York: W.W. Norton & Co., 1991), 2-11.

[19] Cf. Tocqueville, *Democracy in America,* trans. Harvey Mansfield and Delba Winthrop (Chicago: University of Chicago Press, 2000), 29-31 and 42-44.

weak to persist in the world.[20] And it was in the society of these people that Tocqueville discovered a peculiar genius for combining the spirit of freedom and the spirit of religion, so that each was understood to support the other. Indeed, this genius for incorporating the two distinct spirits of the age may very well be that "seed of what is to follow and the key to almost the whole work" to which Tocqueville refers earlier in the chapter.[21] On the other hand, Tocqueville is careful to state that, unlike the mission-minded Puritans of Massachusetts Bay, the colonists of Virginia were *sent*, and arrived in the New World as "people without resources or without [good] conduct."[22] We would do well, then, to remember that it was through recourse to the legal form of the joint stock corporation that *both* Virginia *and* Massachusetts Bay were established in America. Clearly, the legal form of corporation allows for a wide variety of specific determinations.

The Court's first important ruling on the constitutional status of a corporation came in *Dartmouth College v Woodward*.[23] Speaking for the Court, Chief Justice Marshall ruled that private corporations were to be included under the protection of the contract clause. By upholding the colonial era charter, which granted to the trustees control of the private eleemosynary institution in perpetuity, Marshall ensured that the associational rights of the persons who had contributed their capital to the corporation were not violated by the state authorities, who sought to allocate those resources for an altogether different, secular purpose. While corporate law continued

---

[20] John Winthrop, "A Model of Christian Charity" (1630).

[21] Tocqueville, *Democracy in America*, 29. Alternately, we might look to the extensive footnotes Tocqueville provides in the chapter in order to discover a second "key" in the dramatic change in the character of Puritan law over the course of a few generations. Even if we were not to adopt this interpretation of the text, we would do well to remember the prominent role played by Virginians during the American Revolution, Philadelphia Convention, and early years of the Republic.

[22] Tocqueville, *Democracy in America*, 30-31.

[23] 17 U.S. 518 (1819).

to evolve over the next half century, our next stop is the Court's important ruling in *Santa Clara County v Southern Pacific Railroad*.[24] The case is peculiar in the annals of American law, remembered less for its content than for the headnote appended to the report of the case by the Court Reporter, which reads "One of the points made and discussed at length in the brief of counsel for defendants in error was that 'corporations are persons within the meaning of the Fourteenth Amendment to the Constitution of the United States.' Before argument, Mr. Chief Justice Waite said: The court does not wish to hear argument on the question whether the provision in the Fourteenth Amendment to the Constitution, which forbids a State to deny to any person within its jurisdiction the equal protection of the laws, applies to these corporations. We are all of the opinion that it does."[25] According to legal historian Mortan J. Horwitz, the doctrine was far from the constitutional innovation it might seem to be today. For Waite and his Court, the understanding seems to have been that recognition of corporate personhood under the Fourteenth Amendment would serve only to ensure protection of the property rights of the natural persons joined together under the corporate form.[26] This understanding would later undergo substantial expansion during the Lochner Era, followed by a subsequent chastening under the antitrust movement championed by the Progressives.

---

[24] 118 U.S. 394 (1886).

[25] 118 U.S. 394, 396 (1886).

[26] Counsel for Southern Pacific elaborated in his brief: provisions of state and federal constitutions "apply...to private corporations, not alone because such corporations are 'persons' within the meaning of that word, but because statutes violating their prohibitions in dealing with corporations must necessarily infringe upon the rights of natural persons. In applying and enforcing these constitutional guarantees corporations cannot be separated from the natural persons who compose them." Horwitz, 69-70, citing Argument for Defendant at 12, *San Mateo v. Southern Pacific Railroad*, 116 U.S. 138 (1885) (collected in Cases and Points [available in Harvard Law School Library]).

When paired with the incentives provided by I.8.8, the corporate form took on new significance and a new orientation in American society. The corporate arrangement allowed investors to hedge against the dangers which come from investment in new technology: individuals need no longer bear the brunt of failed ventures alone. By spreading their capital across a number of firms, these investors encouraged research and experimentation in a variety of different sectors of the economy. Even the most risk-averse investors were persuaded to invest some of their capital in such ventures, provided the price was right and the firm had established a record for producing returns on investment. In this way, the corporate form helped to ensure a steady supply of capital to fund the efforts of those individuals willing to undertake the difficult and time-intensive work of what we now call research and development. Indeed, it struck an important balance between the bourgeois preference for moderate work, comfort, and stability, and the gambler's high risk / high reward profile, which is required to produce a continuous stream of new and useful applications. The corporate form facilitated a mutually beneficial partnership between these two distinct human types or classes.

The rise of the corporation and its defense in the courts helped to produce the massive societal changes of the late 19th century. Cities grew as more and more Americans left the farm. Self-employment declined, and fewer American workers practiced the entirety of a trade, as the principle of the division of labor worked its way into American society. The growth of the corporate form brought new prosperity to the nation, but along with this prosperity came increased disparities in wealth, and the people responded by pressing their representatives to develop adequate policies to address these changes. The Court resisted these legal innovations for a while, producing the mixed bag of jurisprudence now commonly referred to as the Lochner Court.[27] But if the Court was resistant to such innovations at the state

---

[27] For an important challenge to the generally held belief that Lochner Era jurisprudence was universally hostile to the regulatory legislation

level, it was willing to defer to those legislative responses provided by Congress. These took two forms: 1) the establishment of permanent, independent federal regulatory commissions and 2) the Sherman Antitrust Act and its subsequent amendments. We need only discuss the first here.[28]

In 1887, Congress established the Interstate Commerce Commission. The first of its kind, the Commission blended the powers of the legislative, executive and judicial branches. Its policy was to declare unjust rail rates illegal. And although it lacked the power either to enforce its orders or to set rail rates, nevertheless the rulemaking authority of the Commission placed rail corporations in a difficult position, the nature of which becomes clear when we recall that, three years later, Congress established the Sherman Antitrust Act, which made collusion with other firms in restraint of trade a federal crime. Were the corporations to fix rates or not? In blending the powers of government, weren't these agencies akin to the tyrants described by Montesquieu? Despite this blending of powers, the Court repeatedly condoned the power of Congress to establish such regulatory agencies.[29] Indeed, one could chart the rise and fall of our most prominent political issues throughout the 20th century by plotting out the rise and fall of federal regulatory agency budgets. For a time, aggressive agency oversight of the conduct of corporations, paired with selective and highly strategic enforcement of the antitrust laws by the Court, precluded talk of the rights of corporate persons. In recent years, however, the doctrine of corporate personhood has

---

developed by the states during this period, see Howard Gilman, *The Constitution Besieged: The Rise and Demise of Lochner Era Police Powers Jurisprudence* (Durham, NC: Duke University Press, 1993).

[28] For more on the development of antitrust law, see Herbert Hovenkamp, "Antitrust Policy After Chicago," 84 *Michigan Law Review* 213 (1985) and my *Antitrust and the Supreme Court* (El Paso, TX: LFB Scholarly, 2012).

[29] For an early, significant, and colorful example see the opinion of Justice Sutherland in *Humphrey's Executor v U.S.*, 295 U.S. 602 (1935).

begun to advance.[30] In the *Hobby Lobby* case the Court would have the opportunity to defend this notion once more.

## Comprehensive Legislation and RFRA

One of the primary narratives of twentieth century jurisprudence traces the Court's gradual application of the doctrine of incorporation, which holds that the guarantees of the Bill of Rights may be applied by the courts to strike down state legislation through the due process clause of the Fourteenth Amendment. Let it suffice to say that such a change did take place, as even a quick survey of the Court's rulings during this period would indicate.[31] We take up the story with Justice Scalia's landmark opinion in *Employment Division v. Smith*,[32] in which the Court discarded the strict scrutiny test which had been applied in free exercise cases since *Sherbert v. Verner*. In place of that test, the Court ruled that states need not grant exemptions to religious objectors from neutral, generally applicable laws. Congress responded to the Court's ruling in *Smith* with the Religious Freedom Restoration Act of 1993, which reinstituted the strict scrutiny test adopted in *Sherbert* and discarded in *Smith*. But when asked to apply RFRA in *Boerne v. Flores*, the Court declined to do so, ruling that it was beyond the remedial power of Congress

---

[30] Most prominently in *Citizens United v. FEC*, 558 U.S. 310 (2010), but see also *First National Bank v. Belotti*, 435 U.S. 765 (1978), *FEC v. Wisconsin Right to Life, Inc.*, 551 U.S. 449 (2007), and *American Tradition Partnership, Inc. v. Bullock*, 567 U.S. ___ (2012).

[31] *Reynolds v. U.S.* 98 U.S. 145 (1879); *Cantwell v. Connecticut* 310 U.S. 296 (1940); *Minersville School District v. Gobitis* 310 U.S. 586 (1940); *West Virginia Board of Education v. Barnette* 319 U.S. 624 (1943); *McGowan v. Maryland* 366 U.S. 420 (1961); *Braunfeld v. Brown* 366 U.S. 599 (1961); *Gallagher v. Crown Kosher Super Market of Mass., Inc.* 366 U.S. 617 (1961); *Sherbert v. Verner* 374 U.S. 398 (1963); *Wisconsin v. Yoder* 406 U.S. 205 (1972); *Thomas v. Review Board* 450 U.S. 707 (1981); *U.S. v. Lee* 455 U.S. 252 (1982); *Corporation of Presiding Bishop of Church of Jesus Christ of Latter-Day Saints v. Amos* 483 U.S. 327 (1987).

[32] 485 U.S. 660 (1990).

under §5 of the Fourteenth Amendment to prescribe the standard of review which the Court ought to apply in cases where it is called upon to apply the free exercise clause to state legislation.[33] RFRA could not be used by religious believers to secure exemptions from generally applicable *state* laws, but with respect to the Court's application of generally applicable *federal* laws, the statute remained in place. In 2000, Congress amended RFRA with the Religious Land Use and Institutionalized Persons Act (RLUIPA), which broadened protections for religious believers, making clear that RFRA covers "any exercise of religion, whether or not compelled by, or central to, a system of religious belief," and, important to the disposition of the *Hobby Lobby* case, making clear that the provisions of RFRA applied to all legal persons, natural and artificial.[34]

Ten years later, President Obama signed into law the Patient Protection and Affordable Care Act. One provision of the Act required most group health plans to cover certain preventive-health services without cost-sharing, stipulating that these plans also require coverage, "with respect to women, [of] such additional preventive care and screenings...as provided for in comprehensive guidelines supported" by the Health Resources and Services Administration (HRSA), a component of the Department of Health and Human Services (HHS).[35] Because HRSA did not have such comprehensive guidelines in place at the time, HHS requested that the Institute of Medicine (IOM) develop recommendations. IOM brought together a group of experts, who recommended a number of preventive services, including access to the "full range" of "contraceptive methods" approved by the Food and Drug Administration (FDA). Religious non-profit corporations and for-profit firms employing fewer than 50 individuals were exempt from these requirements, as were all employers who had not yet made any changes to their health plans

---

[33] 521 U.S. 507 (1997).
[34] 42 U.S.C. §§2000cc-5(7)(A) and 573 U.S. ____ (2014) J. Alito, 29-31.
[35] 42 U.S.C. 300gg-13(a)(4) (Supp. V 2011).

since implementation of ACA began. Norman and Elizabeth Hahn and their three sons own Conestoga Wood Specialties, employing around 950 workers to make wooden cabinets. David and Barbara Green and their three children own and operate two businesses, Mardel, a Christian bookstore with 35 stores and roughly 400 employees, and Hobby Lobby, an arts and crafts retailer with 500 stores and roughly 13,000 employees. The Hahns and the Greens filed suit separately with HHS and other federal agencies seeking to enjoin application of the HHS mandate to their closely-held for-profit corporations under RFRA and the free exercise clause.

## Corporation and Regulation, Hobby Lobby and HHS

When viewed from the standpoint of constitutional theory, we see that the case requires the Court to resolve difficulties arising when separate constitutional policies come into conflict with one another. Could there be some way to ensure the protection of religious liberty, make clear the utility of the corporate form, and facilitate the equity perceived to flow from administrative and regulatory oversight of the conduct of those corporations? Such are the problems addressed by constitutional jurisprudence. Justice Alito, in writing for the Court, opted not to tackle the most general question to present itself in the case—whether or not for-profit corporations have a constitutionally protected right to the free exercise of religion, absent further statutory protection from Congress. While other members of the Court majority might have been willing to revisit the precedent established in *Smith* and revise its free exercise jurisprudence, Alito saw no reason to reach the constitutional question, finding in the amended text of RFRA sufficient grounds for providing the exemption requested by the plaintiffs. Justice Alito would seem to be something of a judicial minimalist—he likes to keep his rulings narrow and shallow.[36] To the

---

[36] Cass Sunstein, *One Case at a Time: Judicial Minimalism on the Supreme Court* (Cambridge: Harvard University Press,1999). Cf. the "Ashwander Rules" laid out by Justice Brandeis in his concurring opinion in *Ashwander v. TVA*, 297 U.S. 288 (1936), 346-348.

extent that Justice Alito's opinion for the majority does address the question of corporate personhood, the claims are modest, in the mode of pre-*Lochner* jurisprudence. Corporate personhood is indeed a fiction, but that fiction has an important use.

> [T]he purpose of this fiction is to provide protection for human beings. A corporation is simply a form of organization used by human beings to achieve desired ends. An established body of law specifies the rights and obligations of the *people* (including shareholders, officers and employees) who are associated with a corporation in one way or another. When rights, whether constitutional or statutory, are extended to corporations, the purpose is to protect the rights of these people. For example, extending Fourth Amendment protection to corporations protects the privacy interests of the employees and others associated with the company. Protecting corporations from government seizure of their property without just compensation protects all those who have a stake in the corporations' financial well-being. And protecting the free-exercise rights of corporations like Hobby Lobby, Conestoga, and Mardel protects the religious liberty of the humans who own and control those companies.... Corporations, "separate and apart from" the human beings who own, run, and are employed by them, cannot do anything at all.[37]

While his language does at times suggest that the Court could discover within the text of the First Amendment alone grounds for protecting a corporate right to free exercise, Alito makes it abundantly clear that he is not doing so here. Mardel, Conestoga Wood, and Hobby Lobby are granted their exemptions from the HHS mandate because Congress extended RFRA protection to corporate persons when it passed RLUIPA. Pursuant to the terms of the amended RFRA, even corporations may, upon a showing that a law places a substantial burden on their exercise of religion, require the government to prove to the Court that the law 1) serves a compelling government interest and 2) that the burden to the person is the least restrictive means of furthering that compelling interest. While the Court concedes without examination that the government interest in

---

[37] 573 U.S. \_\_\_\_ (2014) at 18-19.

providing cost-free access to all FDA approved contraceptives is compelling,[38] it finds a number of suitable, less-restrictive alternatives available to Congress, and authorizes the exemption on these grounds, observing that "both RFRA and its sister statute, RLUIPA, may in some circumstances require the Government to expend additional funds to accommodate citizens' religious beliefs….HHS's view that RFRA can never require the Government to spend even a small amount reflects a judgment about the importance of religious liberty that was not shared by the Congress that enacted that law."[39]

In her dissenting opinion, Justice Ginsburg takes issue with this reading of RFRA, dismisses the language of RLUIPA upon which Alito relies, and cites in its place language from Senators Ted Kennedy and Barbara Mikulski to bolster her legal reasoning.[40] The dispute over how seriously the Court ought to take legislative history is unlikely to be resolved any time soon, and I will not attempt to do so here. Perhaps it is sufficient to note that there are those Justices on the Court who prefer to work primarily from the language of the statute itself, and those who prefer to supplement that language with quotes from speeches made on the House and Senate floor, or

---

[38] The peculiar position of Justice Anthony Kennedy as the most prominent 'swing justice' on the Court has been well-documented. In any 5-4 ruling of the Court, it is worth looking into how Kennedy may have used this position to color the language of the majority opinion by threatening to defect unless certain language was added to or removed from the opinion of the Court. Justice Kennedy's sticking point in this case seems to have been getting the Court to acknowledge or concede that the Government's interest is compelling. Justice Kennedy's concurrence draws this point out, and Justice Ginsburg's dissent also seizes on it. Justice Alito downplays the significance of this assumption, since the mandate so clearly fails the second prong of the test prescribed by RFRA. Cf. 573 U.S. \_\_\_\_ (2014) J. Alito, 40; J. Kennedy, concurring, 2-3; J. Ginsburg, dissenting, 24-25.

[39] 573 U.S. \_\_\_\_ (2014) J. Alito, 43.

[40] 573 U.S. \_\_\_\_ (2014) J. Ginsburg, dissenting, 6, 9. Other Senators relied upon to construe the law: Barbara Boxer, Dianne Feinstein, and Patty Murray.

inserted into the legislative record later by Congressional staff. At any rate, it should be observed that all of the language pulled from the record of Congress by Justice Ginsburg to support her reading of RFRA was delivered by members of the Democratic party. While the tendency toward hyperbole[41] on display in Justice Ginsburg's dissent is largely of a piece with the less-than-judicial tone of a statutory interpretation colored solely by quotes pulled from members of one political party, even more important is the manner in which the dissenters largely dismiss or subsume the plaintiffs' argument from religious liberty. For the dissenters, "religious organizations exist to foster the interests of persons subscribing to the same religious faith,"[42] and while they "agree with the Court that the Green and Hahn families' religious convictions regarding contraception are sincerely held" they would rule that those beliefs, "however deeply held, do not suffice to sustain an RFRA claim. RFRA, properly understood, distinguishes between 'factual allegations that [plaintiffs'] beliefs are sincere and of a religious nature,' which a court must accept as true, and the 'legal conclusion…that [plaintiffs'] religious exercise is substantially burdened,' an enquiry the court must undertake."[43]

---

[41] See, for example, Ibid at 13-20 and 32-34. Justices Kagan and Breyer wrote separately to make clear that they did not join the former section of Justice Ginsburg's dissent. In the latter, the dissenters share their concern about the scope of future corporate exemptions, pointing to several extreme examples: exclusion of black patrons from a restaurant, exclusion of young, single women working without father's consent from working at a private health club, refusal to photograph a lesbian couple's commitment ceremony on religious grounds, exemption from covering blood transfusions, antidepressants, pills coated with gelatin and vaccinations. Leaving to one side the judgment upon religious conduct implied when the dissenters liken the conduct of the Greens and Hahns to such cases, it is worth noting that the Court majority refuses to address such concerns until they are properly before the Court in a concrete case, while the dissenters show no such scruples.

[42] Ibid, at 16.

[43] Ibid, at 21-22 (internal citations omitted).

Religious opinion is made to yield before the objective, factual findings of panels composed of scientific experts.

The Court's response to this contention is clear, though perhaps not as elaborate as those looking to the Court for a strong defense of religious liberty would hope: "HHS and the principal dissent in effect tell the plaintiffs that their beliefs are flawed. For good reason, we have repeatedly refused to take such a step."[44] A strong defense of religious liberty would not only tell the reader that there were good reasons for not taking such a step—it would elaborate, providing those reasons and allowing interested citizens and future members of the Court alike to determine whether or not they were indeed good. Indeed, each of the five members of the Court who authored opinions in the case appears ill at ease when speaking in defense of religious liberty in any detail. Notably, Justice Alito spends considerably more time elaborating on the status of benefit corporations[45] than explaining why the Court must continue to refrain from passing judgment on the religious beliefs of the Hahn and Green families. To the extent that the authors of the principal opinions (Alito and Ginsburg) do elaborate on why the Court must continue to protect free exercise, they cast their defense in the language of others—the Hahns and Greens, the opinions of previous Courts, the statutory guidance of Congress. But in the most opportune moments, when the argument calls for a fresh defense of religious liberty from a sitting member of the Court, the Court falls silent.

## On Liberty, Personal and Relational

In recent years the Court has had a great deal to say about the scope and meaning of the liberty enshrined in the due process clauses of the 5th and 14th Amendments, and in the process it has to a great extent rehabilitated the doctrine of substantive due process applied in cases

---

[44] 573 U.S. ____ (2014) J. Alito, 36-37. The context of the claim is also worth noting, though excluded here.

[45] Ibid, 21-24.

as disparate and as universally scorned by contemporary legal scholars as *Dred Scott v. Sandford* and *Lochner v. New York*. In what is likely the most prominent instance of the Court's development of this doctrine, the plurality opinion in *Planned Parenthood v. Casey*, Justices O'Connor, Souter and Kennedy provided a candid account of the substantive concept of liberty they believed to be enshrined in these amendments:

> Our law affords constitutional protection to personal decisions relating to marriage, procreation, contraception, family relationships, child rearing, and education. Our cases recognize "the right of the *individual,* married or single, to be free from unwarranted governmental intrusion into matters so fundamentally affecting a person as the decision whether to bear or beget a child." Our precedents "have respected the private realm of family life which the state cannot enter." These matters, involving the most intimate and personal choices a person may make in a lifetime, choices central to personal dignity and autonomy, are central to the liberty protected by the Fourteenth Amendment. At the heart of liberty is the right to define one's own concept of existence, of meaning, of the universe, and of the mystery of human life. Beliefs about these matters could not define the attributes of personhood were they formed under compulsion of the State.[46]

This is certainly an expansive account of individual liberty. It is also a highly personal account. But this personal and individual account of liberty is incomplete. It leaves out the relational component of human freedom. When the Court speaks of personal or individual liberties without also acknowledging the relational dimension to human freedom, it tells us less than we should know from carefully reading and thinking about our Constitution, and teaches us that we, as free individuals, are left, as it were, naked and alone when called on to assert or embody this freedom before the

---

[46] 505 U.S. 833, 851 (1992) (emphasis added, internal citations omitted).

power of the state.⁴⁷ It is one function of those cases in which legislation is challenged as a violation of our constitutionally protected religious liberty to invite a Court which appears determined to provide substantive protection for liberties through the due process clauses to develop a more adequate account of the character of that liberty, showing that true liberty consists not merely in defining concepts alone, but in sharing those concepts with other free persons.

One reason for the enduring popularity of our First Amendment is that it provides each of us as citizens with an account of what the truth is like, and how it is to be found. Any Court which requires truth-seeking to yield to fact-telling is in sore need of rediscovering the authentic meaning of the First Amendment. Writing more than a century before the American founding, in the same decade that John Winthrop was speaking to his fellow Puritans about how they might model Christian charity for the rest of the world, John Milton indicated the orientation of that liberty of conscience which stands just behind each of the freedoms enshrined in the First Amendment: "And though all the winds of doctrine were let loose to play upon the earth, so Truth be in the field, we do injuriously by licensing and prohibiting to misdoubt her strength. Let her and Falsehood grapple; who ever knew Truth put to the worse, in a free and open encounter? Her confuting is the best and surest suppressing."⁴⁸ The First Amendment requires that Congress, in pursuing its constitutional obligation to make law for the general welfare, may not prohibit the free exercise of religion. The other freedoms delineated in the First—speech, press, assembly and petition—follow from this fundamental proscription. The founders, Federalist and Anti-Federalist together, knew that human freedom would not flourish without protection for

---

⁴⁷ The critique of contemporary substantive due process was suggested by Peter Augustine Lawler, who highlights some of the problems stemming from the highly personal, but not relational, account of human liberty being developed by the Court in recent years in, "Defending the Logos Today," in *Reason, Revelation and the Civic Order*, ed. Paul DeHart and Carson Holloway (Dekalb, IL: Northern Illinois University Press, 2013).

⁴⁸ John Milton, *Areopagitica* (Indianapolis: Liberty Fund, 1999), 45.

the relational component of that freedom. They also knew that it would be folly to attempt to establish this freedom in law—no state can compel us to be free. But as anyone who has sat around the seminar table and spent time engaged in serious discussion of the great books will appreciate, this is an activity open to each of us as persons in relational conversation with one another. While the Court's ruling in *Burwell v Hobby Lobby* fails to make these connections clear, we may still hope that the rights protected by the First Amendment will receive a more spirited defense from the Court in the future.

# 8

# WHAT SORT OF GOD CALLS FOR LIBERTY OF CONSCIENCE?

*Michael Novak*

Many gods have appeared in human history, in all parts of the world. Not all these gods call for liberty of conscience. Nor do all cultures develop institutions to protect liberty of conscience. Why would they? Most of these gods have no use for conscience. Most of the gods who have appeared in history seem remarkably indifferent to any human being's interior life.

Consider four concrete examples.

First, the ancient religions of Greece and Rome asked their followers to keep the formal practices of their locality, city, or people. They did not ascend into the realm of conscience. Christians, however, could not perform these practices without violating their own consciences. Their external actions needed to be at one with their consciences. To burn incense to other gods—even if Christians did not take these other gods seriously—would make liars of themselves. For their God is a God of "Spirit and of Truth," not of external practice merely.

The gods of Greece and Rome laid no stress on such inwardness. However, in *Antigone,* conscience did begin to peep through. Antigone felt from deep within her heart a conflict between what the local pieties demanded she must do in regard to her brother's remains, and what was *right* to do. This is an early appearance of moral conflict between a conscience formed by the traditions of a city/state, and a conscience formed by a duty to one's own rational nature. Some see in this a premonition of *natural rights* deeper than positive law and custom; others, a premonition of conscience. The coming of Christianity to Athens (and to Rome) put

Antigone's moral protest under a new philosophical and religious paradigm, focused directly on Spirit and Truth, not custom nor external *pietas*.

Second, in Syria today, Christian leaders are forced to choose between dhimmitude and death. Under dhimmitude they must pay a ransom twice a year just for being allowed to live (and thus to acquiesce to the Muslim claim to rightful dominion over all other religions). To this extent, they must abjure their previous faith.

In addition, dhimmis are forbidden to make any show of any other religion: not wear religious symbols, not build new churches, not preach on the streets, not distribute religious literature, not make sounds within their meeting places that might be heard outside. Dhimmis are no longer counted as full citizens. They live a half-life. They have bound themselves into self-declared secondariness—under threat of severe bodily punishment or death. Anyone who would die rather than obey these conditions condemns to death not only himself; he also condemns his entire family to diminished rights and freedoms, to extreme hardship, without their breadwinner and male protector. Islam of a certain sort does not allow freedom of religion. It demands submission to the will of Allah.[1]

Third, the ideologically secular culture that is now coming to power in Canada, the U.K., and the U.S. seems to find no reason within itself to protect freedom of conscience for religious persons who do not subscribe to all secular moral views. Florists and photographers whose consciences find it wrong for *them* to serve at same-sex weddings are being heavily punished for following their consciences.[2] So far, very few secular believers speak up for liberty of

---

[1] See Nina Shea, "Syrian Jihadists Are Forcing Christians to Become Dhimmis under Seventh-Century Rules," *National Review Online* (February 28, 2014), accessed March 26, 2014: http://www.nationalreview.com/corner/372283/syrian-jihadists-are-forcing-christians-become-dhimmis-under-seventh-century-rules.

[2] Many competitors stand ready to provide such services, and those being punished make no attempt to prevent others from doing so. The driving motive, therefore, seems compulsion, punitive compulsion.

conscience for Christians whose convictions diverge from secular orthodoxy. Similarly, even in his classic on religious liberty, *A Letter concerning Toleration* (1689), Locke excluded two classes from such liberty: Catholics and atheists. Religious liberty for only some is not religious liberty.

Fourth, the god of deism, yet again, is usually described as impersonal, unfeeling, and indifferent to the individual conscience. Such a god is unmoved by the human fate even of the noble and the heroic. He is said to be like a watchmaker who has wound up the world and lets it move forward by some impersonal, unfeeling and blind evolutionary process. For deism, liberty of conscience is a nonissue.

Worse, one of the easy falsehoods modern historians have allowed to spread is that the founders of the United States—Washington, for example, and the American Congress—were deists, spoke as deists, acted as deists. Thus it follows, according to this argument, that the founders did all their writing within a worldview that had no place for reliance on the personal God of Judaism and Christianity. That would also mean that when they wrote of the sacred rights of conscience,[3] and wrote earlier that the rights to life, liberty, and the pursuit of happiness are "endowed in us by our Creator," they did not mean what they wrote.

Such an illusion does not survive examination of the formal pronouncements of the U.S. Congress (with their accompanying Presidential Proclamations), as we shall soon see. Let us attend first to the prior question. What *is* deism? In *Washington's God*, I have written on this question at length.[4] Here I will summarize.

---

[3] Cf. letter from James Madison to Thomas Jefferson (October 17, 1788), in *The Sacred Rights of Conscience: Selected Readings on Religious Liberty and Church-State Relations in the American Founding*, ed. Daniel L. Dreisbach and Mark David Hall (Indianapolis: Liberty Fund, 2009), 413.

[4] For further precisions on the distinctive nature of deism, the belief that by rational methods alone men can know all true propositions of theology, etc., see Chapters 6 ("What's a Deist? The Deist Tendency") and 7 ("Not a Deist, but Judeo-Christian") of Michael Novak and Jana Novak,

Deists of the period 1775-1800 held that their god cannot intervene in human history, that prayer is of no avail to humans, and that the deist god has nothing at stake in what happens to humans. Deism does not have a prescribed body of doctrines or even practices. It is more like a tendency, an ever-shifting drift of ideas, across two or three generations. *The Dictionary of the History of Ideas* lists ten propositions that fluidly and loosely were signs of the deist tendency. Not all these propositions were held by all. Yet the *Dictionary* noted that one of them, number five, defines the basic point that has led some historians to call the founders deists:

> 5. There is no special providence; no miracles or divine interventions intrude upon the lawful natural order.

Now, did any founding father affirm this proposition #5? I have not found a single founder who did so, although Jefferson may have come closest.

Almost alone among the top hundred founders of the American republic, Jefferson had a tendency toward deism (or Unitarianism, as deism's formal institution was called). In its spirit, he published the *Jefferson Bible*, which scissored out from the New Testament all the miracles recorded therein, in order to pass on only the *moral teachings* of "the most sublime" moral teacher of all time, as Jefferson called him, Jesus Christ.

Indeed, Jefferson asserted more than once that the New Testament is the best of all moral teachers for the virtues necessary to

---

*Washington's God: Religion, Liberty, and the Father of the Country* (New York: Basic Books, 2006), 95–118, 119–142. There we note the propositions from *The Dictionary of the History of Ideas* that deists have generally subscribed to, including #5 noted here: "That there is no special providence; no miracles or other divine interventions intrude upon the lawful natural order" (110). The latter marks a decisive break from the Judeo-Christian tradition. On the issue of how deism in history has worked out as a stepping stone toward atheism, see also Avery Cardinal Dulles, "The Deist Minimum," *First Things* (January 2005), available at http.://www.firstthings.com/article/2005/01/the-deist-minimum.

republics: honesty, conscientiousness, responsibility, initiative, industry, and especially self-control and self-government. His motive for preparing the *Jefferson Bible* was to have it spread, at federal expense, to instruct the Indians of the new Louisiana Territory in how to prepare themselves for life in a republic.

But not even Jefferson was a consistent deist. He *did* think that the Almighty acted in history. He *did* believe that there is a divine Governor of human events. He did believe that the Almighty reads human consciences and judges them—not just outward behaviors, but inner temptations and decisions. Listen to the language of Jefferson's Declaration:

> We, therefore, the Representatives of the united States of America, in General Congress, Assembled, appealing to *the Supreme Judge of the world for the rectitude of our intentions*, do, in the Name, and by Authority of the good People of these Colonies, solemnly publish and declare, That these United Colonies are, and of Right ought to be Free and Independent States.[5]

It is not hard to see why men in the age of Newton and other scientific giants might feel a bit more comfortable talking a philosophical language about God (the Almighty, Governor, Providence, Judge, Creator) than the less scientific-sounding, merely storytelling language of the Hebrews and earlier Christians. The language of science sounded more sophisticated. And Newton's own habit of speaking without discomfort both as a scientist and as a Christian reassured others that both languages could be spoken at the same time. The Jewish-Christian God is a God of Reason, Law, Logos (as, by contrast, the Islamic God is a God of pure will alone[6]).

In a parallel vein, the most detailed historian of human liberty, Lord Acton, argued that institutions of liberty of conscience are

---

[5] "The Declaration of Independence, July 4, 1776," available at: http://www.archives.gov/exhibits/charters/declaration_transcript.html.

[6] Cf., for example, Norman L. Geisler and Abdul Saleeb, *Answering Islam: The Crescent in Light of the Cross* (Grand Rapids, Mich.: Baker Books, 2002), 140.

*coincident* with the history of Judaism and Christianity. Why is this plausible? Because Judaism and Christianity conceived of God not as an idol of stone or gold or silver or wood; and not, either, as a dark panther of the jungle, nor a python, nor the force of rain as in Central and South America; nor again as an anthropomorphic and mythical cavorter with the fate of humans (such as Zeus, Jupiter, Neptune, Venus, Apollo, and a cloud of others); nor as the polytheistic legions of Hinduism. Jews and Christians spoke (and speak) of God as *Spirit and Truth*, the *Creator* and *undeceivable Judge* and *Governor of events*.

This is the God of history, Who invites humans to purity of conscience, friendship with Him, and love for one another and for Him. The Jewish and Christian God is the only one on Whom the signers of the Declaration of Independence could plausibly call to testify to "the rectitude of our intentions." The Jewish and Christian God is the God of Spirit and Truth, Who sees into consciences and knows their innermost valleys and crevices. St. John the Evangelist describes the words of Jesus on the differences between the gods of Samaria, the traditional Jewish God, and the new order that Jesus is announcing: "But the hour is coming, and is now here, when true worshipers will worship the Father in Spirit and truth; and indeed the Father seeks such people to worship him. God is Spirit, and those who worship him must worship in Spirit and truth."[7]

The intention of the American patriots was not rebellion, they insisted, but the upholding of principles once shared by the Crown—it was George III who was now in rebellion against those principles. They called on the Almighty to judge the truth of their own consciences in this regard.

Furthermore, the top hundred American founders[8] were not deists. Every one of them, including Jefferson and Franklin, spoke of

---

[7] John 4:23-24.

[8] On the top hundred or so American founders, a group I take to include the signers of the Declaration of Independence and the signers of the Constitution, see the full discussion in "The Forgotten Founders," the

God as their Creator Who endowed rights in them, the Governor of all events, the Providence solicitous for them, their Judge. Nonetheless, a disbelief in miracles and in divine interventions (special providence) characterizes deists and distinguishes them from Christians and ancient Hebrews. By this criterion, were the official proclamations and laws of the early U.S. presidents and Congresses deist or Christian?

## The First Argument: The Public Acts of Congress and Presidents

Many are the historians of recent decades who have spread abroad that the founders of these United States were deists. The best test of whether that is actually true is to produce studies of the religious convictions and practices of the top hundred founders of the nation—the eighty-five who signed either the Declaration of Independence or the Constitution, or both, plus a few others such as Tom Paine, Abigail Adams, George Mason, and so on. Professors Daniel L. Dreisbach and Mark David Hall have well begun this research, not only in *The Sacred Rights of Conscience*.[9]

Yet in a sense the private convictions and practices of each of these founders, while fascinating, are not as weighty as their official, corporate actions as legislators and presidents. In importance to the United States of America, their *official acts* trump their private beliefs and actions. Nowhere are their official acts more accessible—in relation to religious matters—than in the decrees and proclamations promulgated by presidents and successive Congresses. During the twenty-five founding years (1774-1799), on more than twenty public and official occasions, either the Congress or the president (or both) made official declarations about the indispensability of religion (of the Jewish/Christian type) for republican governments. For example, they

---

appendix of Michael Novak, *On Two Wings: Humble Faith and Common Sense at the American Founding* (San Francisco: Encounter Books, 2002), 127–58.
[9] Cited above. See n. 299.

often urged the *states* to conduct days of thanksgiving, or repentance and fasting, and other such public religious acts.

Were we to examine just which actions the many congresses expected *God* to perform in order to respond to these nationwide prayers, we could test immediately whether the founders were deist or Jewish/Christian.[10] From a massive body of texts, I here single out only two documents.[11] The first came early in the founding period, and the second came at the end of the War of Independence. The first is the Proclamation of the National Day of Humiliation, Fasting, and Prayer of the Second Continental Congress of June 12, 1775.

> As the great Governor of the World, by his supreme and universal Providence, not only conducts the course of nature with unerring wisdom and rectitude, *but frequently influences the minds of men to serve the wise and gracious purposes of his providential government*, and it being, at all times, *our indispensable duty devoutly to acknowledge his superintending providence, especially in times of impending danger and public calamity,* to reverence and adore his immutable justice as well as to implore *his merciful interposition for our deliverance...*

[There, in added italics, three times in the first sentence are lines incompatible with Deism. The document goes on...]

> This Congress, therefore, considering the present critical, alarming and calamitous state of these colonies, do earnestly recommend that Thursday, the 20th day of July next, be observed, by the inhabitants

---

[10] Incidentally, as often as possible, the founders preferred to use names for God and his attributes provided by the Jewish Testament rather than the Christian. This was a neat way to appeal to something all believers shared, whether Christians or Jews, whether Trinitarians or Unitarians, whether Protestant of Catholic, whether evangelical or Anglican, whether biblical or, like Tom Paine, a rational, commonsense believer in God.

[11] In *Washington's God* and *On Two Wings: Humble Faith and Common Sense at the American Founding*, I have collected pointed texts that most shocked me out of my assumptions about the deism of the founders, and referred readers to anthologies of sermons of the founding period. There is now a metastasizing body of documents from the founding era, in which searchers can examine mountains of newly available evidence.

of all the English colonies on this continent, as a day of public humiliation, fasting and prayer; that we may, with united hearts and voices, *unfeignedly confess and deplore our many sins*; and offer up our joint supplications to the all-wise, omnipotent, and *merciful Disposer of all events*; humbly beseeching him to *forgive our iniquities*, to remove our present calamities, to avert those desolating judgments, with which we are threatened, and to bless our rightful sovereign, King George the third, and [to] *inspire him with wisdom to discern* and pursue the true interest of all his subjects, that a speedy end may be put to the civil discord between Great Britain and the American colonies, without farther effusion of blood: *And that the British nation may be influenced to regard the things that belong to her peace*, before they are hid from her eyes: ... *That virtue and true religion may revive and flourish throughout our land; And that all America may soon behold a gracious interposition of Heaven, for the redress of her many grievances, the restoration of her invaded rights, a reconciliation with the parent state, on terms constitutional and honorable to both; And that her civil and religious privileges may be secured to the latest posterity.*[12]

It would be fantastical to regard this resolution of the Congress as a deist document. There is not a line in it that would give comfort to a deist. However, on that point note an interesting twist. In the founding generation, many Christians, even bishops, also employed a deist language as a way of speaking about God philosophically. Then they also used the language of the Bible, to make a parallel argument in biblical terms. They were fond of drawing comfort from the complementarity of the two arguments.[13]

Many Roman Catholics *in addition to the Bible* also cherish the ancient Greek and Roman humanistic concepts, and the philosophies of essence and existence centuries later developed from them. To make sense of the world, many Protestants in the founding period also availed themselves of the more abstract language of deism, but

---

[12] Cf. *Journals of the Continental Congress, 1774-1789*, ed. Worthington C. Ford, Gaillard Hunt, et al., vol. 2 (Washington, D.C.: Government Printing Office, 1904-37), 87-88.
[13] An interesting aside: Most deists in America were men; women seemed to prefer the more personal language of biblical religion.

without surrendering their biblical faith. Indeed, they typically found biblical faith and commonsense reason complementary, like the two wings of an eagle. Especially in sermons on solemn civic occasions, arguments for liberty in the founding period were most often made twice: once in biblical terms, and again in philosophical terms, as in Locke and Sydney.

The second text is the Congressional Resolution calling for "A Day of Thanksgiving and Prayer" (October 18, 1783).

> Whereas it hath pleased Almighty God, the Father of all mercies amidst the vicissitudes and calamities of war, to bestow blessings on the people of these states, which call for their devout and thankful acknowledgments, *more especially in the late remarkable interposition of his watchful providence, in rescuing the person of our commander in chief and the army from imminent dangers, at the moment when treason was ripened for execution; in prospering the labors of the husbandmen, and causing the earth to yield its increase in plentiful harvests; and, above all, in continuing to us the enjoyment of the gospel of peace.*
>
> It is therefore recommended to the several states to set a part Thursday, the 7th day of December next, to be observed as a day of public thanksgiving and prayer; *that all the people may assemble on that day to celebrate the praises of our Divine Benefactor; to confess our unworthiness of the least of his favors, and to offer our fervent supplications to the God of all grace; that it may please him to pardon our heinous transgressions and incline our hearts for the future to keep all his laws; to comfort and relieve our brethren who are any wise afflicted or distressed; to smile upon our husbandry and trade; to direct* our public councils, *and lead our forces, by land and sea, to victory;* to take our illustrious ally under his special protection, and favor our joint councils and exertions for the establishment of speedy and permanent peace; to cherish all schools and seminaries of education, *and to cause the knowledge of Christianity to spread over all the earth.*[14]

---

[14] *Journals of the Continental Congress, 1774-1789*, ed. Worthington C. Ford, Gaillard Hunt, et al., vol. 18 (Washington, D.C.: Government Printing Office, 1904-37), 950-51.

Do not these two official Resolutions spell out clearly enough the worldview, beliefs, and religious actions of the founding generation? Are they deist or Christian? One can inspect similar texts in an almost unbroken chain down through the time of Abraham Lincoln and on into the 1950s.

## From a Duty to the Almighty, to a Right before Men

Some argue that deists set aside biblical concepts such as Creator, Judge, Governor, and Savior but, nonetheless, maintain a doctrine of religious liberty because of their commitment to reason and the human individual. That may be.

But that is *not* the argument made by Thomas Jefferson in his *Bill for Religious Liberty* nor by James Madison in his *Remonstrance*. Both men argue from the character of a Creator in relation to his creatures, and from the nature of the Creator as no mere idol of stone or precious metal, but a Living God Who is Spirit and Truth, an undeceivable Reader of human hearts.[15]

Here is the way the argument of Jefferson went.

> *Almighty God hath created the mind free*; [and] all attempts to influence it by temporal punishments or burdens, or by civil incapacitations, tend only to beget habits of hypocrisy and meanness, and are a departure from *the plan of the Holy Author of our religion, who being*

---

[15] As an even stronger example, Tom Paine was not a deist, but a theist. He was a debunker and ridiculer of much in the Bible. But he most strongly believed in a God of Spirit and Truth, and in an endowment in each human being by the Creator of natural rights. Paine even took ship to France in 1789 to urge the Revolutionaries not to turn to atheism, lest they lose the firmest ground for natural rights. No one tells this tale more sympathetically to Paine than Harvey Kaye of the University of Wisconsin, Green Bay, in his book *Thomas Paine and the Promise of America* (New York: Hill and Wang, 2005).

Lord both of body and mind, yet chose not to propagate it by coercions on either, as was in his Almighty power to do.[16]

Jefferson's argument in favor of liberty of individual conscience, then, goes like this. A person's liberty of conscience is based on the intention of the Creator to make every human free, and to endow in each a duty. This duty is the self-evident duty of any conscious creature to pay gratitude and worship to his Creator. Given this freedom, each individual person has a duty to be grateful and to worship—but *in the way* that her conscience directs. (Her conscience, moreover, is not static, but changes with learning and experience.)

Since each human person is endowed with capacities for insight (questioning, *What is that?*) and judgment (questioning, *But is that true?*), each must worship according to his own judgment as to the most fitting manner of doing so. For the Lord, although He did not have to, created the mind free, and so He wishes it to remain.

Madison gave this argument three deeper, more solid twists: The *right* of conscience springs from a *duty* to the Creator; if a duty to God, then a right before men—an unalienable right; and this right is precedent to family, civil society, and state. For it springs from a universal Sovereign, Who stands above all social bonds.[17] Madison wrote:

> [W]e hold it for a fundamental and undeniable truth, "that religion *or the duty which we owe to our Creator* and the manner of discharging it, *can be directed only by reason and conviction, not by force or violence.*"

---

[16] "A Bill for Establishing Religious Freedom, 18 June 1779," available at: http://founders.archives.gov/documents/Jefferson/01-02-02-0132-0004-0082.

[17] Here Catholic philosophy goes further than Madison: it identifies union with God as the common good of all human beings, all united in one. It highlights the reality of universal communion, and avoids imagining that the seat of rights lies in the lonely individual. Yet at the foundation, it affirms that the base of rights is the equal communion of all persons in God, together with the freedom of each person to accept or to reject God's offer of communion.

> The Religion then of every man must be left to the conviction and conscience of every man; and it is the right of every man to exercise it as these may dictate. *This right is in its nature an unalienable right.* It is unalienable, because the opinions of men, depending only on the evidence contemplated by their own minds *cannot follow the dictates of other men*: It is unalienable also, because what is here a right towards men, *is a duty towards the Creator.* It is the duty of every man to render to the Creator such homage and such only as he believes to be acceptable to him. *This duty is precedent, both in order of time and in degree of obligation, to the claims of Civil Society. Before any man can be considered as a member of Civil Society, he must be considered as a subject of the Governour of the Universe:* And if a member of Civil Society, do it with a saving of his allegiance to the Universal Sovereign.[18]

To summarize, the essence of the argument goes like this: it is self-evident that a creature owes not only gratitude to her Creator (to Whom she owes everything she has), but also worship (given the infinitely different level of power on which the Creator operates). Otherwise, what an ingrate a creature would show herself to be. And what a pretentious and self-blinded creature she would be, not to be in awe of greatness far beyond her own measure.

When the creature perceives her duty to worship in Spirit and Truth, no one else dare stand in the way of her fulfilling that duty. For she owes that duty both to the Almighty, and to herself. And if she has such a duty to her Creator, then she also has the right to fulfill it—in which no one dare interfere—not the state, nor the civil society, nor mother, nor father, nor brothers or sisters, nor any other being. That right is unalienable in two directions, toward God and toward men.

In sum, Madison and Jefferson made an essentially Jewish and Christian argument for religious liberty. The God of Judaism and Christianity does not wish the worship of consciences to be coerced,

---

[18] "Memorial and Remonstrance against Religious Assessments [ca. 20 June] 1785," available at: http://founders.archives.gov/documents/Madison/01-08-02-0163.

that is, to regard them as slaves, but of free women and men who choose to respond affirmatively to His offer of friendship.

This view does not mean that in order to enjoy this liberty, a citizen must be a Christian or Jew. On the contrary, since all humans are creatures of this Creator, this God of Spirit and Truth, all share in this liberty equally. Jews and Christians do not claim this liberty solely for themselves, but recognize that it belongs to all. Jews and Christians have a principled argument for defending the liberties of those who reject God and excuse themselves from his friendship. Do secular thinkers have a principled ground for recognizing the liberties of those who believe in the God of spirit and truth? It appears not, at least at this time.

Nonetheless, to see how this liberty came to be recognized in history, eventually even institutionalized in history, it is highly useful to grasp its Jewish and Christian provenance. It is also useful to see what a long historical pilgrimage was required to grasp its full implications, and to experiment with ways to conceive of it clearly and, after many attempts and failures, to institutionalize it securely.

For the sake of emphasis, let me re-state the above to make my point crystal clear: I have been able to find in no other religion a reasoned defense of the liberty of conscience of others. I have encountered no secular philosophy that successfully does so without relapsing into relativism, which makes a mockery of all reason. So far as I can see, few ideologically secular actors stand up for the consciences of Christians and Jews. By contrast, Christians and Jews in the path blazed by Jefferson and Madison have given every reason why the mind of secular actors is by nature free, and their rights to intellectual liberty are also unalienable. Christians and Jews have done for the secular, what so far the secular have not been able to do for them.

## Conclusion

Madison and Jefferson knew full well that what they were conceptualizing and beginning to institutionalize were "the fabrics of governments which have NO MODEL on the face of the globe."[19] Their mature ideas eventually issued from a new science of politics,[20] one not yet worked out in prior history. But that very notion of "progress" in history ("Thy Kingdom *come* on earth") was a Christian concept. History under Judaism and Christianity, was *not* what it had been for the ancients, a cycle of endless return. Neither was it a straight line up or down. Rather history is, as it were, an upwardly biased spiral of highs and lows, including periods of decline and then recovery.[21] History represents the upward progress, slow and subject to many abrupt declines, of the actions and achievements of free women and men.

For Christians, life is to be conceived not as a tragedy (although many awful tragedies appear in it) but, in the end (as Dante grasped), a comedy. The last word is with divine friendship—in Dante's words, "the Love that moves the sun and all the stars." William Penn of the Society of Friends then insisted: "If friendship, then also liberty." Thence, the Liberty Bell of Philadelphia. The Lord God Creator made sure that at least one type of creature on earth—each human being—could become conscious of all He has done, give thanks, and freely accept (or reject) His proffered friendship.

---

[19] *Federalist* 14.
[20] See *Federalist* 9.
[21] The Second and Third Awakenings.

# INDEX

Aarsleff, Hans 82n
Abraham 25, 27, 28, 40, 42
Acton, Lord John Dalberg 163-4
Adair, Douglas 140n
Adam 13, 15
Adams, John 107
Aeschylus 20
Alexander, Bishop of Alexandria 45
Alexander the Great 42
Allen, Pauline 47n
Alito, Samuel 133, 150-1, 154
Alypius 50
Amar, Akhil Reed 140n
Antieau, Chester J. 105n
Arius 45
Ashcraft, Richard 82n
Athanasius 48-9
Athanassiadi, Polymnia 20n, 37n
Atra-Ḫasīs 12, 16, 19
Augustine of Hippo 127-8
Avi-Yonah, Michael 50n
Barnes, Timothy 45n, 47n
Bayle, Pierre 93
Beiner, Ronald 94n
Bellah, Robert N. 87-8
Belz, Herman 143n
Beneke, Chris 66n
Berger, Warren 70-1
Berman, Joshua 24n
Berman, Harold 18n
Berns, Walter 92n, 124n, 125n
Bidez, Joseph 37n
Black, Hugo 113-4
Boggs, Lilburn (Governor of Missouri) 67
Bossy, John 80n
Bowersock, G.W. 50n, 51n
Brandeis, Louis 142
Brant, Irving 140n

Breyer, Stephen 153n
Burke, Thomas Carroll 105n
Caesar, Julius 42
Calvert, Cecilius 3, 63, 72-3, 76-82
Calvin, John 74, 77n
Carr, Lois Green 79n
Carroll, Phillip Mark 105n
Carter, Stephen L. 119
Celsus 43n
Charles I (King of England) 77
Claiborne, William 79
Clark, Tom 70
Conley, Patrick T. 65n, 66n
Constantine (Emperor of Rome) 36n, 37, 38, 44, 45, 48-49, 52, 60n
Constantius (Emperor of Rome) 47, 48, 58, 59
Crèvecoeur, J. Hector St. John de 67-8
Cromwell, Oliver 77
Cullen, Daniel 3-4, 87, 94n
Cyril of Alexandria 43
Cyrus (King of Persia) 22, 32
Daniel 52
Dante (Alighieri) 173
David (King of Israel) 24, 42
Derathé, Robert 95n, 100n
Digeser, Elizabeth 36n
Dionysus 46
Drake, H.A. 36n
Downey, Glanville 47n
Dreisbach, Daniel L. 105n, 108n, 109n, 110n, 118n, 165
Dulles, Cardinal Avery 162n
Dwight, Timothy 68
Dworkin, Ronald 91n
Eisenhower, Dwight D. 87
Eliot, T.S. 9n

Elliott, T.G. 50n
Enki 12, 16, 19
Enlil 15, 16, 19
Ephrem Syrus 52, 53n
Epstein, David F. 140n
Euripides 20
Eusebius of Nicomedia 38n, 45, 52
Eustathius, Bishop of Antioch 47-8, 55
Euzoius, Bishop of Antioch 47-8, 55
Farrelly, Maura Jane 3, 63, 67n, 73n, 77n, 78n
Finke, Roger 67n, 68n
Finkelman, Paul 66n
Flanders, Robert G. Jr. 66n
Ford, Bridget 68n
Foster, Benjamin R. 11n
Fox, Edward 78n
Franklin, Benjamin 164
Frede, Michael 20n
Frohnen, Bruce 88n
Frolov, Serge 24n
Geisler, Norman L. 163n
George III (King of England) 164, 167
George, Bishop of Cappadocia 57
Gilden, Hilail 89n, 94n
Gilgamesh 32
Gillespie, Michael Allen 140n
Gilman, Howard 147n
Ginsburg, Ruth Bader 152-4
Goliath 42
Goodstein, Laurie 69n
Goodwin, Daniel C. 67n
Gordon, Thomas 107n
Gourevitch, Victor 94n
Graham, Michael 78n
Greenawalt, Kent 91n, 93n
Greenhouse, Linda 64n
Gregg, Sam 17n
Gregory of Nazianzus 52
Grosby, Steven 2, 9

Grotius, Hugo 26n
Gunn, T. Jeremy 112n
Habermas, Jurgen 92n
Hadrian (Emperor of Rome) 50
Hall, Mark David 165
Hamburger, Philip 113n
Hamilton, Alexander 136n
Hanson, R.P.C. 46n, 47n
Harbison, Winfred A. 143n
Hartley, William G. 67n
Hatch, Nathan O. 67n
Hazony, Yoram 25n
Heidegger, Martin 142n
Herodotus 10
Hesiod 10, 20
Hillel II 50
Holmes, Oliver Wendell Jr. 103
Horwitz, Morton J. 143n, 145
Hovenkamp, Herbert 147n
Hughes, John 66
Huldah 24
Hume, David 54
Hunter, James Davison 92n
Ingle, Robert 79
Isaiah 22, 29
Jacob 42
Jay, John 107, 136n
Jefferson, Thomas 35n, 61-2, 71-2, 80-1, 84, 103-5, 108-11, 113, 125, 126n, 162-4, 169-72
Jeremiah 27, 29
Jesus of Nazareth 38, 40, 43-46, 53, 57
Job 27, 28
John the Evangelist 164
Johnson, Curtis, D. 68n
Josephus 43n
Josiah 24
Julian (Emperor of Rome) 2-3, 35-62
Kagan, Elena 153n
Kant, Immanuel 54n, 61-2
Karmann, Thomas 47n

# INDEX

Kaye, Harvey 169n
Kelly, Alfred H. 143n
Kelly, George Armstrong 88n, 100n
Kennedy, Anthony 152n, 155
Kennedy, Edward 152
Kessler, Sanford 72n
Lactantius 35n, 104n
Larsen, Mogens Trolle 12n
Lawler, Peter Augustine 156n
Licinius (Emperor of Rome) 36n
Lienesch, Michael 140n
Lloyd, Gordon 65n
Locke, John 3, 35n, 63, 72-3, 77, 80-5, 89, 99, 161, 168
Lombrozo, Jacob 77
Lowenthal, David 90n
Lycurgus 56
Machiavelli, Niccolo 53-4, 55, 60n
Machinist, Peter 21n
Madison, James 35n, 54, 71, 81, 90n, 108, 112, 118, 125, 127, 136n, 140, 142, 161n, 169, 170-2
Maier, Pauline 140n
Main, Jackson Turner 140n
Manent, Pierre 127n, 130
Marcellinus, Ammianus 36n, 44, 46, 47, 50n, 57-9
Marduk 19, 20
Marshall, John 134, 144
Marx, Karl 54n
Masters, Roger D. 89n
Maxentius (Emperor of Rome) 38
Mayer, Wendy 47n
McConnell, Michael W. 91n
Meese, Alan J. 133n
Meletius, Bishop of Antioch 47-9, 55
Melzer, Arthur 91n
Meyer, Arnold Oskar 78n
Mill, John Stuart 35n, 62
Milton, John 35n, 156

Mikulski, Barbara 152
Montesquieu, Charles-Louis de Secondat 54, 55n, 56, 136, 147
Morgan, Edmund S. 74n
Moses 40-2
Muñoz, Vincent Phillip 88n
Murray, John Courtney 87n
Naboth 24
Nathan 24
Nee, Laurence D. 81n
Newdow, Michael 63n
Newton, Isaac 163
Nichols, Joel A. 104n
Niebuhr, Gustav 67n
Nieves, Evelyn 64n
Nilsson, Martin P. 19n
Noah 12-15, 26
Nock, A.D. 37n
Noll, Mark A. 66
Novak, Jana 161n
Novak, Michael 5, 87n, 159, 161n, 165n
Obama, Barack 149
O'Connor, Sandra Day 155
Oman, Nathan B. 133n
Owen, J. Judd 81n
Owen, John 35n
Paine, Thomas 169n
Paul 44n
Penn, William 173
Peter 41
Philostorgius 46n, 50n, 53
Pliny the Elder 43
Pliny the Younger 43n
Plutarch 56n
Porphyry 43n
Prothero, Stephen 69n
Pythagoras 56
Ramsey, David 5, 133, 147n
Ravitch, Diane 67n
Rawls, John 92n
Riordan, Timothy B. 79n

Rousseau, Jean-Jacques 3-4, 87-100, 123
Russell, Jeremiah H. 2, 35
Saleeb, Abdul 163n
Samson 42
Scalia, Antonin 148
Scholasticus, Socrates 46n
Scruton, Roger 89n, 99n
Selden, John 26n
Semele 46
Shea, Nina 160n
Shepardson, Christine 47n
Sherover, Charles M. 94n
Shils, Edward 10n
Smith, George 11
Snell, Daniel C. 30n
Socrates 56
Souter, David 155
Sozomen 46n, 49n
Stark, Rodney 67n, 68n
Stern, Andrew H.M. 68n
Stewart, Potter 119
Stoner, James R. Jr. 139n
Storing, Herbert J. 140n
Strauss, Leo 82n
Sunstein, Cass 150n
Sutherland, George 147n
Sydney, Algernon 168
Tacitus 43n
Tertullian 35n
Theodoret 47n, 50n, 51n, 59n
Thomas, Clarence 111
Thucydides 10, 56
Titus (Emperor of Rome) 40, 50
Titus, Bishop of Bostra 57n
Tocqueville, Alexis de 4, 87n, 96n, 97, 121-4, 127-131, 143-4
Trenchard, John 107n
Troeltsch, Ernst 17n
Underwood, William 1n
Voltaire 35n
Waite, Morrison 145
Walton, Reggie B. 64n
Warburton, William 93
Warren, Samuel 142n
Washington, George 64-5, 67, 71, 88, 92, 105, 122-3, 126-7, 128n, 161
West, M.L. 20n
William III (King of England) 80
Williams, Roger 3, 35n, 63, 72-7, 79
Winthrop, John 144n, 156
Witte, John Jr. 1n, 4, 89, 90, 103, 104n, 108n, 112n
Wohl, Alexander 70n
Yenor, Scott 4, 121, 126n
Zosimus 58n
Zuckert, Michael 82n, 124n

*The Most Sacred Freedom* includes eight essays that were first presented at the 2014 A.V. Elliott Conference on Great Books and Ideas, the seventh annual conference sponsored by Mercer University's Thomas C. and Ramona E. McDonald Center for America's Founding Principles. Together, these essays explore the great principle of religious liberty by charting its development in the Western tradition and reconsidering its place at America's founding.

The book begins with a comparison between the flood accounts in Genesis and the Mesopotamian *Atra-Hasis* and advances all the way to the 2014 Supreme Court case *Burwell v. Hobby Lobby*. The intervening chapters examine the contributions of figures such as Emperor Julian, Roger Williams, Cecilius Calvert, John Locke, Jean-Jacques Rousseau, and the American Founders.

The major themes addressed include the theological and epistemological preconditions of religious liberty, the chief challenges to securing this liberty, the problematic but necessary role of religion in a free society, and the constitutional framework that has been handed down to us to help preserve this most sacred freedom.

Contributors to the volume are Steven Grosby, Jeremiah H. Russell, Maura Jane Farrelly, Daniel Cullen, John Witte, Jr., Scott Yenor, David Ramsey, and Michael Novak.

*Will R. Jordan is an associate professor of Political Science at Mercer University. He received his BA from Washington & Lee University and his PhD in Political Science from Loyola University Chicago. Jordan also serves as codirector of Mercer's McDonald Center for America's Founding Principles.*

*Charlotte C. S. Thomas is a professor of Philosophy at Mercer University, director of the Philosophy, Politics, and Economics program, and codirector of the McDonald Center for America's Founding Principles. She received her BA from Mercer University and her PhD in Philosophy from Emory University.*

Essays / Philosophy

Mercer University Press
1501 Mercer University Drive
Macon, Georgia 31207
www.mupress.org
Cover design: Burt&Burt
Cover art: Library of Congress